THRIVE

ELIMINATING
LACK
FROM YOUR LIFE

BY RICHARD ROBERTS

RICHARD ⊕
ROBERTS
ORAL ROBERTS MINISTRIES

Copyright © 2019
By Richard Roberts
Tulsa, OK

ISBN 978-1-7325385-1-1

Published by Oral Roberts Evangelistic Association
P.O. Box 2187
Tulsa, OK 74102-2187
All rights reserved.
Printed in the United States of America.

TABLE OF CONTENTS

PRINCIPLE 3: SOWING

CONCLUSION

INTRODUCTION

Over thirty years ago, my father, Oral Roberts, wrote a book titled *Attack Your Lack*. When he first wrote the book and taught the message within it, it was a revolutionary concept. The idea that believers could go into spiritual warfare against the attack of the devil in order to live the abundant life God has planned for us was a new way of thinking for so many Christians.

Let me tell you, that groundbreaking message is just as essential and life-changing for Christians today as it was when my father first shared it. Over the years, Oral Roberts Ministries has received millions of letters, phone calls, and emails from people asking for prayer. And we still continue to get thousands of messages each day by phone, email, and social media from people who are desperate for the God-given breakthroughs that can come to us through the power of prayer.

Throughout the history of this ministry, the main prayer requests we've received have been spiritual, physical, financial, or family-related. But whatever circumstances you may be facing, the approach my father taught for getting your needs met was always the same. He approached every situation — spiritual, physical, financial, family-related or anything else — by "attacking the lack."

Whenever Satan has come to steal, kill, and destroy (John 10:10), my father considered it his mission in life to help believers experience the rest of that scripture, which says, "But Jesus came to give us life and life more abundantly."

In fact, one of my father's favorite scriptures was 3 John 2, *Beloved, I pray that you may prosper in all things and be in health, just as your soul prospers.* The word *prosper* here means to have a successful journey on the road of life, a prosperous and expeditious journey, led by a direct and easy path. The word *health* means to be sound, to be well, to be strong. The word *soul* speaks of our mind, will and emotions. It includes your feelings and desires.

This is God's highest wish for our life. He desires that we would be prosperous, successful, healthy, well adjusted, content, and strong in every area as we journey through life. In fact, Dad felt 3 John 2 was such a complete scripture for healing that it was part of his daily prayer routine. And for many years that scripture has been a part of my prayer routine, too.

In other words, because of what Jesus already accomplished when He went to the Cross on our behalf, we as believers have a Bible right to attack our lack and expect to begin to thrive in God's abundance, in Jesus' Name.

That's the approach that my father took. And it's the approach that my wife, Lindsay, and I have taken and continue to take when dealing with the devil's tactics — *because it works.* We know it works. We've seen the miraculous results firsthand in our lives.

When Lindsay recently received a vicious diagnosis of cancer, we were faced with two choices. We could let the devil continue to attack us, or we could use our faith, apply the Word of God to the situation, and attack our lack. We chose to attack our lack. I went to a toy store, bought Lindsay a small, yellow rubber duck, and said to her, "You are not a sitting duck waiting for the other shoe to drop and more bad things to happen. You are the righteousness of God in Christ Jesus." And *you* have a Bible right to begin to thrive in God's abundance.

That day, Lindsay and I went on the attack. We went after the devil. We went after the cancer — by faith. We pursued healing

— by faith in God's Word, and with medicine as well. And I am grateful to say Lindsay is now cancer-free.

I'll say it again — we went on the attack. And I want to declare to you that you can go on the attack too. You can do it right now, no matter what is facing you. You are not a sitting duck, waiting until the enemy, the devil, comes to devour you. As a blood-bought believer in Christ, you have a Bible right to come against your needs, in faith, and expect God to bring about a breakthrough for you. By faith, you can begin to thrive.

CHAPTER ONE

What Is the Real Problem?

What is the most urgent problem facing you today?

When I ask people this question... when I invite people to share their needs with me so I can pray for them... people invariably talk to me about many types of needs. They mention spiritual needs like feeling far from God or temptations that they have fallen into and need forgiveness for. They talk about physical needs like healing from cancer, heart problems, asthma, diabetes, chronic pain, and other sicknesses and diseases. They say they need jobs, increases in salary, and freedom from debt. They mention broken relationships with spouses, children, parents, and friends. They ask for prayer because they are worried, discouraged, or depressed.

But let me ask you this. What is at the root of these problems? What is the real problem that lies underneath these prayer requests? Thousands of people write or call our ministry every month. They contact us, asking for prayer for the needs they are facing. And at the root of every prayer request they make is one question:

"Can God really help me? How can I get my needs met — spiritually, physically, financially, and in my family — while I'm living on this earth? How can I have my needs met and also be a witness for Christ and carry on His work at the same time? How can I really thrive in His abundance? Is this even possible?"

So many times in our ministry, we hear Christians say things like, "The minute I get one need met, something else happens. How am I ever going to get ahead?" The people reaching out to us come from every walk of life. But one thing they all have in common when they contact us for prayer is that they are facing a need.

Often, the needs we face can seem totally overwhelming, and they can make it hard for us to see the positive things in our lives. Like a storm cloud blocking the sun, our needs can seem to hide God and His promises from our view.

When our focus is on the challenges we're facing in our lives — when we're consumed with what we lack — it can fill us with fear and anxiety. We can end up fighting so much doubt that we may even question if God can help us. We may find ourselves wondering if He is listening to us when we pray.

No matter what situations we are facing, if we're not experiencing the miraculous blessing of having our needs met, then we can become worn down in our inner man. We can become frustrated and discouraged because the need just won't go away.

We may ask, "Why has this happened to me? What have I done to deserve it? Why me? Is there something wrong with me?" We may start to wonder how anyone can make it in a world filled with unbelief, sickness, disease, lack, broken relationships, sadness, fear, and so many other challenges. We may even say to ourselves, "I guess God doesn't have the answers for me. I might as well give up."

Unanswered Needs Can Lead to Doubt

If this describes you or someone you know… if you're feeling so down in your inner man that you wonder if you'll ever get up again… then I have a message for you. Don't give up! I want you to consider this…

Satan comes to steal, kill, and destroy, according to John 10:10. When you're facing a need, the doubter of all doubters, the father of all lies, Satan, will show up. He tries to cloud your thinking with thoughts like these: "Being a blood-bought Christian doesn't seem to be doing me much good. Maybe walking with the Lord doesn't pay off. My coworkers and neighbors don't even know You, Lord, and yet they are getting their needs met better than I am. God, where are You?"

Do you know when I believe Satan attacks us the hardest? I believe he does his best to try to get us to doubt God in times when need wears away at us… when we're facing need after need after need hammering away at our faith and joy… day after day… week after week… sometimes even year after year.

Sometimes, it's hard to be honest with ourselves and others about how the lack in our life is wearing us down. Many times, as Christians, we find ourselves putting on our "game face." We try to appear, from the outside, as if we have it all together. But on the inside… fear, doubt, and worry are trying to creep in. We may have figured out how to hide our real feelings and thoughts from others. But if we're not getting our needs met by God, then the fear, the hurt, the frustration, and the pain will continue to haunt us.

And that's when Satan tries to slip into our lives to cause confusion and discouragement. That's when it can seem as if the great sermons you hear aren't reaching down to where you live. The powerful, prophetic Word of God may not seem to be relevant to your everyday needs. The Spirit-filled music you used to love so much during worship may not seem to get you excited about God anymore. Your prayer life can suffer. And you find yourself asking, "Why is this happening to me? Why doesn't the devil leave me alone?"

During such times, the devil will try to convince you that nothing is happening in your life, that nothing is going to change, and that God doesn't care about you.

But I'm here to tell you that nothing could be further from the truth! God cares for you! When God said in 3 John 2, *Beloved, I pray that you may prosper in all things and be in health, just as your soul prospers,* He wasn't saying that just for my father, Oral Roberts. He wasn't just saying it for me, a minister of His healing power. That verse isn't just for mighty prophets or anointed pastors and ministers. It's for you! It's for every blood-bought child of God.

God wants you — yes, you — to prosper and be in health in every area of your life. God doesn't want you to lack any good thing.

So, when you find yourself asking if God still does today what He did for people in Bible days, the answer is a resounding YES! Where are such mighty men and women of God today? Friend, look in the mirror! Who can get a prayer through to Heaven in the times we live in? You can — by faith! Can you really expect a miracle to happen to your life, your physical body, your finances, your family, and your spiritual life?

I believe God's answer to you is yes, yes, YES! He wants you to thrive in His abundance.

Why We So Often Struggle

You may be asking, "Richard, if God cares for me, then why am I still facing needs and lack? If God is telling me I can expect a miracle, then why am I struggling with my circumstances right now?"

I believe the answer lies in the difference between how Christians are meant to approach our circumstances and how the world wants us to approach them.

Think for a moment about what life is like today. Television, the Internet, and all the other conveniences available can make it seem as if everything in our lives should be easy. They provide instant answers to us. Turn on the TV, and you'll get instant entertainment. Watch the ads, and they'll claim that if we just buy the right food, the right clothes, and the right car, our lives will be wonderful.

Meanwhile, in the realities of life, we're faced with all sorts of challenges that may seem to be never-ending. Sickness may affect us or someone we love. We receive a bad report from the doctor. The job market gets bad, or there are layoffs. Bills pile up. The car breaks down. There's too much month left at the end of the money. The news is filled with crime, violence, war, and fear.

We're surrounded in this world by so much negativity… so much fear and doubt. And while it's true that Satan is at work attacking people and causing lack in their lives, I believe God has a solution for us. I believe with all my heart that He wants us to go on the offense against the work of the devil. I believe God wants us to attack our lack. Instead of letting our needs rule over us, we are to come against them in faith and see those needs met by God's mighty power. That's living in abundance!

Let's look at John 10:10 again more closely. Notice what the scripture says: *The thief does not come except to steal, and to kill, and to destroy. I have come that they may have life, and that they may have it more abundantly.*

Do you see that? Yes, it's true, Satan has a job. But so does Jesus. The Lord's job is to give Christian believers *life* — life more abundantly. The word *life* here in this verse is not the Greek word "bios" — it's not life solely in the sense of natural, biological, physical life. It's more than just existing and breathing.

You see, the word Jesus used as He said what He said in John 10:10 is "zoe" — a Greek word that describes the God-kind of life, a life filled with every good and perfect gift God has planned for us (James 1:17).

And here's something else you should know about this verse. The word *abundantly* in John 10:10 doesn't just mean "a lot" or "much." It means "over and above, more than necessary, supremely, something further, much more than all, extraordinary, surpassing, uncommon and more excellent." That sounds like a miracle to me. And Jesus is the miracle worker!

Pay close attention here… If we as Christians begin to understand the ways of Jesus and how He operates, I believe that's when the miracles will begin in our lives. Matthew 6:33 says, in essence, "Seek first the kingdom of God and His ways of doing and being (His ways of operating in the kingdom). Then all the things you have need of **shall be added to you**." That's what I call living in God's abundance.

Notice, too, that these scriptures are all about our life here on earth. They're talking about the world we live in today, not the Heaven we're going to someday. In Matthew 6:9–13, Jesus explains to His disciples how to pray. We are to pray for God's kingdom to come and His will to be done on earth, just as it is done in Heaven.

He also said we are to pray that God would give us *this day our daily bread*. Jesus was making reference to God's supply being provided for us here on earth. He did not say we should wait to have our daily needs met when we get to Heaven. He was talking about the kingdom of God coming to earth. In fact, Jesus brought the kingdom of God to the earth to demonstrate it for us… to show us how God operates or His ways of being and doing.

According to Jesus Himself, God is well able to bring His kingdom to this earth and supply our daily needs. Miracles are for today, for right here and right now. Here on earth is where people hurt, where people lack health, money, friends, and hope. Right here and now is where the need is. This is where the battle is.

And this is where we can overcome lack through faith, and through God's Word.

3 Biblical Principles for Overcoming Lack

You may be asking, "But Richard, how do I overcome my lack? Is there a biblical way of living so that I can walk in abundance and prosperity? Are there key principles of increase I can apply and know they will work for me?"

Yes! There is something you can do — even in the midst of your need — to put yourself in position to expect and receive miracles. I believe there is an answer, according to the Word of God, for how we can walk in victory instead of defeat, in abundance instead of lack. As you reach out and pick up the Bible, I believe that you can find an answer that will speak directly to you at the point of your need.

I have found in my studies of God's Word, and in living by faith in my own life, that there are principles to follow. These three biblical principles to overcoming lack in our lives are so simple at their heart. And I believe they will work for any

Christian who will act on these principles by taking a step of faith, beginning right now.

Principle 1 — Believe

Everything we accomplish in life starts with our faith. Fortunately for us, the Bible tells us that God has given to every person the measure of faith (Romans 12:3). We all have the faith we need to begin believing God for miracles.

The scriptures also say that the just shall live according to their faith (Habakkuk 2:4, Romans 1:17, Galatians 3:11, and Hebrews 10:38). And Hebrews 11:1 says, *Faith is the substance of things hoped for, the evidence of things not seen.* The word *substance* in this verse means "a firm foundation, steadfastness of mind, courage, and resolution." In other words, faith in God is our firm foundation. It is what we stand on as we believe that God will do what He said He will do, even though we may have not seen the evidence yet.

So, what are we to believe?

First, we are to believe that God is a *rewarder*. Hebrews 11:6 says that we must believe that God is, and that He is *a rewarder of those who diligently seek Him*. Many people believe that God exists, but if we're going to experience miracles and see our needs met, we must go a step further. We must also believe that He rewards us when we diligently seek Him by faith.

Second, believe in yourself. Philippians 4:13 says, *I can do all things through Christ who strengthens me.* In our own self, we might doubt our abilities. But as a believer, we can add "through Christ" into the equation, and that changes the situation.

Remember, Peter failed as a fisherman until Jesus got in his boat — and then he had a net-breaking, boat-sinking haul of fish. Lazarus was dead until Jesus commanded him to come forth from the grave. Saul was persecuting Christians until Jesus confronted him, and then he was converted and ultimately wrote approximately two-thirds of the New Testament while professing the Lordship of Jesus.

Just as Jesus transformed them, He can transform our lives too. He can give us the strength we need for the situations we face. And when we join forces with Him, "through Christ," we can begin to see the miraculous.

Third, expect a miracle. Beginning in the 1950s, my father declared the revelation that God gave him to "expect a miracle." And this revelation is so powerful, if only the Body of Christ will catch hold of it. If Satan had his way, we would continue to expect doom and gloom, devastation, sickness, disease, and anything else he throws our way. But through Christ, the miracle worker, we have a right to expect a miracle according to our faith.

Principle 2 — Speak the Word

The power of words to bring about changes in our circumstances is something that the Bible talks about from the very beginning. Genesis chapter 1 teaches us that God spoke the world into existence with His words. What does this mean for us?

First, realize that our words, when spoken in faith, can bring about changes in our situation. Mark chapter 11 tells us that Jesus taught us to speak to our mountain of difficulty, command it to be cast into the sea, and not doubt in our heart, but believe that those things which we say shall come to pass, in harmony with God's Word and His will. And if we'll do that, we shall have what we say. *Whatever things you ask when you pray, believe that you receive them, and you will have them,* according to Mark 11:24.

Second, we are responsible for what we say — especially what we say in faith. Because our words are so powerful, we are to be accountable for our words and what we say. As Proverbs 18:21 says, *Death and life are in the power of the tongue, and those who love it will eat its fruit.* The *Message* Bible says it this way: *Words kill, words give life; they're either poison or fruit — you choose.*

Third, through our words, we can choose what we agree with. Joshua 24:15 says, *Choose for yourselves this day whom you will serve.* We are to make a choice. What will our words serve — life or death? Who will our words serve — God or the devil? We can choose life and speak life, or we can choose something else. The *power of the tongue* means the power attached to those words. Instead of giving power to the words of the devil, we can use our words to speak the Word of God and activate His power in our life.

Principle 3 — Sow Toward Your Miracle

Luke 6:38 says, *Give, and it will be given to you: good measure, pressed down, shaken together, and running over will be put into your bosom. For with the same measure that you use, it will be measured back to you.* I like to call this a boomerang scripture. What we give comes back to us, and it comes back to us multiplied.

As you act on this principle, keep these truths in mind:

First, choose carefully what you sow. As Luke 6:38 tells us, *Give, and it will be given to you.* Now, this scripture does not distinguish between good and bad seed. Galatians 6:7 says, *Do not be deceived, God is not mocked; for whatever a man sows, that he will also reap.* This verse clearly says, *whatever a man sows.* The law of sowing and reaping applies to *all* seeds, not just the ones that are positive.

When you sow something good, you have a Bible right to expect something good in return. So, it makes sense to sow good things, so that we can receive more of those good things back into our life.

Second, expect a harvest — because a harvest is going to come in due time. Galatians 6:9 says, *And let us not grow weary while doing good, for in due season we shall reap if we do not lose heart.* Genesis 8:22 says, *While the earth remains, seedtime and harvest, cold and heat, winter and summer, and day and night shall not cease.*

As human beings, we can do nothing to stop day from turning to night. We can't keep summer from turning to winter. These are natural laws that operate regardless of what human beings do. The same is true of seedtime turning into harvest. Just as day turns to night and night turns to day, seedtime leads to harvest time. Seedtime and harvest is a natural law, a principle of God. It's an absolute in God's kingdom. The Bible is clear that as we sow out of our need, Jesus is the Lord over the harvest.

Finally, God Himself is the one who brings about the harvest of our believing. In Matthew 13:24, Jesus said, *The kingdom of heaven is like a man who sowed good seed in his field.* There is something very miraculous about a seed. It has life within it. But to bring that life forth, the seed must first be sown. A seed doesn't become a seed until it is planted.

Philippians 4:19 talks about sowing into God's kingdom and reaping a supply of all of our need — *And my God shall supply all your need according to His riches in glory by Christ Jesus.* Acting on this principle of sowing, in faith, enables our giving to turn into receiving. And God becomes our rewarder.

I believe that when we understand the true principle of giving to God, tithing according to His Word, planting seed into His kingdom, sowing into others and even sowing into ourselves, it kickstarts our sowing to turn into reaping.

BELIEVE

CHAPTER TWO

There Is an Answer to Your Lack

The question is, "Can I receive a miracle? Is it possible for me to have my needs met and my lack filled in this world? Is it possible for me to thrive in God's abundance? And if so, how do I do it?"

The answer is yes! There *is* an answer, and it's available to all who will believe God for the answer — including you and me! This is the first thing we must understand and believe if we're going to receive miracles to change our circumstances.

Jeremiah 29:11 (AMPC)

For I know the thoughts and plans that I have for you, says the Lord, thoughts and plans for welfare and peace and not for evil, to give you hope in your final outcome.

God is real, He loves you, and He has answers for your every need. And here's even more good news — *God is not a man that He should lie* (Numbers 23:19). He means exactly what He says in Philippians 4:19 — *My God shall supply all your need according to his riches in glory by Christ Jesus.* He has a supply for the needs you're facing.

But are you tapping into that supply? Do you realize that you *can* tap into His miraculous, overflowing supply for your life?

I believe we have a Bible right to take control of any situation that we find ourselves in. We have a Bible right to take a stand in faith against our circumstances, and begin to attack our lack. We can declare over ourselves that we are moving forward every day, by faith.

I encourage you to make this confession over yourself and your life every day. Start right now and say it out loud: "I believe in God's Word. I believe He loves me. I believe He has answers for me. I can do it! I can overcome and be victorious over the mountain of need I'm facing. I can do it by faith. I will do it, because God is the source of my strength, and He's helping me do it."

You see, if you can begin to believe the Word of God is true, then you can begin to believe that God still speaks today and that He can speak to you if you will take time to listen. When you believe Jesus died and rose again and is closer to you than your breath, then you can begin to understand that He is with you right now, no matter what you're facing.

Your Faith Is the Foundation

Can you see why your faith, your believing, is the first key to attacking your lack and positioning yourself to receive a miracle? When you believe in your heart that God exists, that He is at work on this earth, that He is your rewarder when you seek Him with your whole heart, that He will multiply the seeds you sow, that He will meet you at the point of your need with a miracle... then you can begin to stand in faith to receive from Him. You can begin to declare, "Greater is He who is in me than Satan, the devil, who is in the world."

When you believe with your heart that God is your rewarder here on earth, then you can know that He wants to meet you at the point of your need right now, not just when you get to Heaven, but right now, where you live. And that's when you can begin to discover God's ways to meet your needs, time after time.

Remember, Philippians 4:19 tells us that Jesus is the supplier of *all* our need. That means *every* need, not just some of them.

If God promises to supply *all* our need, then why do so many Christians doubt it? Many people have asked me over the years, "Richard, I know God can meet our needs, but will He meet *this particular need* I'm having?" They wonder if He cares about or has solutions to their specific need. Why do they doubt it, when God has already given them the answer in Philippians 4:19?

We can be tempted to doubt God's supply because of how powerful our need can seem when we're looking it right in the eye. For example, if a person is alone and they don't have friends and family around them, that's a lack. And as a result, loneliness will try to move in and take over. It can make the person begin to confess, "I don't have any friends who care about me." And because our words are powerful and we can receive whatever we are confessing, this loneliness can become a self-fulfilling prophecy in our lives.

Or perhaps we are confronted with something else that's a challenge, like medical bills, worry, financial problems, a diagnosis of sickness, or something else that creates an even bigger lack. It may even seem as if the only thing that is arriving in our life to fill the emptiness is more trouble, more needs, and more lack. Not only are we lonely, but now we are also in debt or depressed or sick. When we have a lack, whatever it is — physical, financial, relational, spiritual — that lack can be like a vacuum in our life. It can feel like our life is so empty in that area, it's all we can think about.

I believe the devil often operates this way, trying to continually attack our lives, trying to use any lack we're facing as an entry point to strike at us. We must be aware of the devil's tactics as we take our stand in faith against our lack.

Remember, John 10:10 says that Satan comes to steal, to kill and to destroy, but Jesus has come so that we might have life, and life more abundantly than we have it right now. If we stop at the first part of that scripture — the part where it tells us Satan comes in to destroy us — then lack will continue to have a path into our lives. The problems will keep coming.

But don't forget about the "but" in that verse. It's such a small word, isn't it? Yet it is such an important word here. Yes, Satan may come to steal, kill and destroy, but Jesus said we are to take note that there's more to the story! Jesus came to turn the bad news of what Satan is doing into the good news of what God is doing! He came to give us life and life more abundantly.

Make Your Decision to Move Forward

What we do about this is up to us. We must make the choice to resist our lack and pursue the abundant life that Jesus came to give us. What does it mean to decide to actively pursue abundant living? It's a lot like a story my friend, Jerry Savelle, shared with me.

Jerry was driving through western Kansas to preach. Now, western Kansas grows a lot of wheat, and the fields were ripe for harvest. After Jerry finished preaching, he decided to drive back to Oklahoma City. And as he drove at night on a lonely highway, he looked ahead of him and saw some headlights. He thought it was an oncoming car, but it wasn't.

As he came nearer, he realized that it was a combine. A farmer was out in his field at midnight. While all the other farmers were asleep, this man was aggressively going after his harvest. Now, that's what I call the right attitude toward attacking our lack and getting our needs met, by faith.

Attacking your lack means you are making the choice to tell the devil, "No, you will not continue to steal, kill and destroy." It means that you choose to take Jesus at His Word and believe for "life and life more abundantly." It means you aggressively go after your harvest, expecting it and looking for it every day.

Remember These Principles

- As Christians, we have a Bible right to take a stand in faith against our circumstances and begin to attack our lack.

- Jesus is the supplier of *all* our need. That means *every* need, not just some of them.

- Jesus came to turn the bad news of what Satan is doing into the good news of what God is doing!

- We can move from lack to thriving in God's abundance.

CHAPTER THREE

We Attack Our Lack with the Faith We Already Have

Have you ever wondered how God sees your situation? Let me share with you four powerful, Bible-based truths that reveal exactly how God sees both our lack and our faith as the way to meet our needs and help us thrive in His abundance.

1. God sees us as being set free from lack.

God has declared in His Word that, as His children, we "lack for nothing" (1 Thessalonians 4:12). Psalm 23:1 tells us that "with the Lord as our Shepherd, we shall not want." What does this mean? It means God is on our side. He doesn't want us to suffer from lack and all the subsequent challenges that arise when we have unmet needs.

2. God sees us as having a supply to meet our needs.

According to Philippians 2:30 and Philippians 4:19, God has set in motion the power to supply our need — not just a portion of it, but all of it. I believe He desires to reveal to us His ways of providing for our needs according to His riches in glory by Christ Jesus. So, it is no accident that you are reading this book. I believe it is part of God's provision for your life because as you allow the truths in this book to get down into your spirit, they can bring forth faith in you. And through it, you can begin to get into a position to receive God's supply for your needs.

3. God's Word tells us that, as His people, we can believe and have our needs met.

Deuteronomy 2:7 says, *For the Lord your God has blessed you in all the work of your hand… the Lord your God has been with you; you have lacked nothing.* Acts 4:34 says that after Jesus' death, resurrection, ascension, and His sending the Holy Spirit, "*neither was there any among them [the disciples] who lacked.*"

Through these and other scriptures, God is showing us that when His people believe that He will meet their needs, He does it. And as a result, they "lack nothing." In other words, God is reminding us that it is possible, through faith in Him, to overcome lack and have our needs met in this life. It is possible not just to survive, but to thrive.

4. God sees your faith as an essential key to your freedom from lack.

God is the source of our supply. And He has provided the way for us to put ourselves into a position to receive what we need. What is that way? It is our faith. As Matthew 6:32–33 says, *Your heavenly Father knows that you need all these things. But seek first the kingdom of God and His righteousness, and all these things shall be added to you.* As we seek Him and put our faith in Him, He will add to our lives the things that will provide for our needs and fill the areas in our lives where we have experienced lack.

You Already Have the Faith You Need

You may be saying, "How do I get enough faith to believe for a miracle?" You may even be feeling like you have no faith.

But Romans 12:3 says that God has given to every person the measure — the necessary measurement — of faith. If we are believers in Jesus Christ, then according to the Bible, we *already* have the faith we need to believe His Word and trust Him to meet our needs. That includes you and me!

What do we have faith in? Well, actually, it's not faith in some*thing*; it's faith in some*one*. Our faith is in a good God, who is the source of a believer's life.

Remember what Hebrews 11:6 says: *He who comes to God must believe that He is, and that He is a rewarder of those who diligently seek Him.* Our believing is to have two parts—believing there is a God, and believing that God is good. And according to Romans 12:3, He has already given to us the measure of faith we need to believe.

Let me say that again, so you can catch what I'm saying. You and I have the ability, the capacity, to believe that God is — that He exists — because according to His Word, He has already given us the ability to believe He exists. In addition to this, He clearly declares that He has given us the ability to believe He is a rewarder. He has dealt to each of us the portion of faith it takes to believe He rewards us when we trust in Him, when we *know that we know that we know* that He is our God, and we earnestly seek after Him!

Our faith is the part of our being that seeks after and responds to God and the things of God. It's our faith at work when we feel a longing to talk to God and hear from Him. It's our faith that stirs in us a desire to please Him, to serve Him, to worship Him and experience His presence in our lives. Through our faith, we can find the will to do things God's way.

Our faith is alive inside our inner man, and it's the part of us that believes God's Word... believes that Jesus is our Lord and Savior... believes that God can make a way for us when there seems to be no way… Our faith is the part of us that believes that God exists, that He loves us, that He is always God no matter how our circumstances appear, and that He has miracles for us if we'll continue believing until we see those miracles come to pass.

Faith is a powerful, living, active, God-given tool that Christians like you and me can use to come against our lack and defeat the attack of the enemy in our lives. And when I say it's active, what I mean is that when we are using our faith to believe God, it doesn't mean we are passive, sitting back, waiting for God to rescue us. Faith is active. It acts.

And why wouldn't we want to take an active stand against our enemy, the devil? After all, he is continually seeking ways to steal, kill and destroy. The devil is actively looking for needs to throw at us. He attacks us with sickness, disease, and lack. And his attack will continue if we don't do something purposeful to resist it. The good news is, we can resist the devil until he flees from us. James 4:7 says, *Submit to God. Resist the devil and he will flee from you.* One Bible version even says the devil will flee from us *in terror.*

As we actively use our faith against the devil, he will flee, and God gives us the victory! God intends for us to win!

So, I encourage you right now to begin believing and declaring, by faith, that you are a victor over your circumstances. Say aloud right now: "I already have the faith I need to expect miracles from God. And I will use that faith, starting now, to resist the devil. I will use my faith to come against the lack in my life and by faith, I believe my needs are met. I believe my needs are met, in Jesus' Name!"

Remember These Principles

- In God, we lack nothing. God has more than enough supply to meet our every need.

- He has already given us the faith we need to believe Him for miracles.

- We can actively use our faith to come against negative circumstances and experience miracles.

- When we resist the devil with the faith we already have, he flees from us in terror.

CHAPTER FOUR

Taking on Overwhelming Odds by Faith

In 2 Kings 6:24–7:20, we learn about an overwhelming siege against God's people, and an amazing miracle that happened when a few humble men were willing to make a move in faith to meet their needs.

At the time, the king of Syria was looking for ways to come against the nation of Israel. So, he sent the mighty Syrian army to surround the city of Samaria. The people of the city were shut up inside the city walls, slowly being starved to death by the Syrian blockade. The resulting famine grew so terrible that people became desperate to survive. Some of them even began to eat the flesh of their own children.

Yet in the midst of this terrifying, horrific situation, five men rose up on the inside and made a faith move toward their deliverance. These five men went on the offense to find a way out of their circumstances. And I believe what these men did is an example to us of how to make a move, in faith, to receive a turnaround in our situation, no matter how desperate it may seem.

Make a Decision to Get Up

Who were these five men? Well, one of them was someone whose name you'll probably recognize if you've studied the Bible. I'm talking about the man of God, the prophet Elisha. The other four are men whose names we don't know, because the Bible never reveals their names to us. All we know is that they were lepers.

These four lepers were sitting outside the city of Samaria, near the gate. Elisha was inside the city. But all of them were affected by the terrible siege. And all of them did something that gave God an opportunity to work through them to do a miracle.

According to 2 Kings 6, the famine and its effects grew so awful, so brutal, that the king of Israel grew angry enough to threaten to put Elisha to death. But instead of yielding to fear or giving up, Elisha turned to the Lord. He called upon God and received a powerful word of deliverance. He boldly said to the king and the people: *Hear the word of the Lord. Thus says the Lord: "Tomorrow about this time a seah of fine flour shall be sold for a shekel, and two seahs of barley for a shekel, at the gate of Samaria."*

In other words, the prophet Elisha had a word from God! He was in essence saying, "In 24 hours, God is going to send us His deliverance. The food that is so scarce right now is going to be so abundant tomorrow that you'll be able to buy all the flour and barley you need for mere pennies."

One of the king's officers didn't believe the word of the Lord that Elisha, the man of God, was sharing with everyone. He said, *"Look, if the Lord would make windows in heaven, could this thing be?"* Another version of the Bible (the NIV) says it this way: *"Look, even if the Lord should open the floodgates of the heavens, could this happen?"*

Elisha replied to the man's negativity and unbelief with

another word from the Lord: *"In fact, you shall see it with your eyes, but you shall not eat of it"* (2 Kings 7:2).

I believe that what God was really saying to the king's officer was this: "If you choose to hold onto your doubt, if you insist on staying negative in the midst of your circumstances, then you won't receive anything to meet your needs. You may even see everyone else around you getting blessed, but you won't enjoy it yourself." In fact, the man would actually die before his time because of his lack of faith.

But it was his choice to make. And it is our choice to make as well. Will we doubt God? Will we stay negative in the midst of trouble and trials? Or will we stand in faith? Will we believe what God says? It is up to us.

Stay in Faith, Even When Things Are at Their Worst

While the prophet Elisha is in the middle of telling the king and all his men the word of the Lord that promised deliverance to the city, the four lepers were seated at the city gates. They had absolutely no idea what Elisha knew. They didn't know God had declared a word of deliverance through the prophet.

As far as these four men knew, they were doomed to die. Because they were lepers, they were not allowed inside the city. They had to beg for all their needs to be met. They depended on the people who went in and out through the city gates to give them food and money for their needs.

But now that the city was under siege, no one was traveling in and out of the city on a regular basis, as they used to do. Everyone in Samaria was trapped inside the city. The lepers were trapped outside the city. And no one had any food, except for the invading Syrian army.

Talk about being stuck between a rock and a hard place! These men must have felt desperate, frightened, and discouraged. No doubt they were starving and weak in their physical bodies. But notice how they approached their situation — because it will reveal an essential key to overcoming challenges.

"Why Sit We Here Until We Die?"

Like a lot of people, these four men were stuck in the middle of a situation that felt like a trap. Their situation was life and death serious, and they didn't have an obvious solution for getting out of it. They were sitting there, in the middle of their circumstances. And if they continued to sit there, they would have remained stuck there until they were dead.

But something suddenly shifted inside of them. Something rose up inside of them, and they asked each other, "*Why are we sitting here until we die? If we say, 'We will enter the city,' the famine is in the city, and we shall die there. And if we sit here, we die also. Now therefore, come, let us surrender to the army of the Syrians. If they keep us alive, we shall live; and if they kill us, we shall only die*" (2 Kings 7:3–4).

Do you see what happened? These men were stirred up by a supernatural plan from God, and they didn't even realize what God was doing. All they knew was that they had an important revelation that we all need to have when our circumstances look bad:

"Sitting here is not going to help us. The only way we might get our need met is to get up and do something about it."

So, the four lepers rose up and walked toward the Syrian army's camp.

A March of Faith Can Lead to Miracles

Remember that these four men didn't know what God had spoken through Elisha. They didn't have the hope of a word from God to guide them. They didn't have a hope of overcoming the Syrian forces, or even that the Syrian soldiers would take pity on them. All they knew was that they had to actively do something, anything, to come against their lack, or they would die.

Sometimes, when we must rise up against our own circumstances, we may not have a lot of hope to go on. But even the tiniest bit of our faith, if we'll act on it, can produce results. Our faith in God and His Word can be the start of our march toward our deliverance.

As these four hungry, sick, outcast men approached the camp of the Syrians, it was nighttime. The soldiers lay asleep in their tents. They weren't expecting or afraid of an attack because the Samarians were trapped inside their city.

But God, who never sleeps, saw the faith of the four lepers. He saw that they had faith enough to do something about their situation. He saw they were believing that He might help them find some food. And through that small act of faith, God was able to move in their circumstances. He sent forth His angels into the Syrians' camp.

The Syrians suddenly awakened to what sounded like the noise of a mighty, conquering army, complete with horses and chariots, ready to attack! The noise they heard was so loud, the scriptures say that the Syrians thought it was actually two armies — the Egyptians and the Hittites — teaming up against them. In a panic, the Syrians fled, leaving everything else behind.

When the four lepers arrived, the Syrian army's camp was abandoned. All the soldiers were gone. Everything the lepers had lacked — food, gold, clothes and more — was there, just ripe for the taking. After they ate and gathered gold and silver for themselves, they hurried back to the city to tell everyone that the Syrians were gone.

It was 24 hours after Elisha gave the word of the Lord to the king of Israel. The people of Samaria rushed out to the enemy's camp and gathered up the spoils. Food was suddenly so abundant that it only took pennies to buy it, just as Elisha had predicted. And sadly, the king's officer, the one who had doubted God's word, was caught in the press of the crowds and was trampled to death.

What Does This Mean for You Today?

No matter what your circumstances may be right now, no matter what need you are facing, there is hope for you… hope in God… just as there was hope for the city of Samaria and the four lepers.

I believe God is at the point of your need, and He is more concerned about you than you can ever imagine. He cares more about you than you may realize. His plans for you are good, plans filled with hope for your future (Jeremiah 29:11). He cares about meeting your needs. That's how good God is! He gets no pleasure out of seeing you lacking any good thing. And He has made a way for you to experience abundance in every area of your life.

I encourage you to read the account of the siege of Samaria, Elisha, and the four lepers in 2 Kings 6 and 7 for yourself. As you do so, keep in mind that these men began to march toward the enemy *before* God turned the situation around by causing the Syrian army to flee in panic. These men acted on their faith *first*. Then — and only then — did God move in to do a miracle on their behalf.

And just as we see in the life of these four lepers, I believe that as you release your faith first and move forward in faith against your needs, God will then begin to move in your circumstances and bring about miracle after miracle in your life.

Remember These Principles

- Your circumstances don't dictate your deliverance. Your faith does.
- Don't focus on what your situation looks like. Remember, God can move on your behalf, even in the worst of times.
- If you stay stuck in your circumstances, they won't improve.
- You must make a move in faith first, before you see a change.
- When you move in faith, then God can move.

CHAPTER FIVE

How a Mother's Faith Attacked Lack — and Won!

To help you get a picture in your heart and mind of what it looks like to successfully attack your lack and thrive in God's abundance, I'd like to tell you a story that I heard my father, Oral Roberts, tell hundreds of times. It's an amazing example of the power of our faith to open up answers to our needs.

The Boy without a Hip Socket

Many years ago, during one of my father's healing crusades in Jacksonville, Florida, a mother stepped into the healing line, and came up before my father to request prayer. She had a son who had a terrible lack in his life — the boy had been born without a hip socket. So, this mother came to my Dad and asked him to pray and believe that her son would be healed.

My father said that it was difficult for him to picture God answering that prayer, because he was used to praying for healing, but the mother was asking for a creative miracle. There is a difference between the two. A healing is the restoration to wellness of something in our physical body that has been damaged or weakened by sickness or disease. A creative miracle, though, is something else — it happens when God creates something that has never been there before.

Now, Dad had a powerful healing ministry at the time. He knew what God's Word said about healing. He knew the Bible tells us that we can pray for "the sick to recover" and for "the Lord to raise them up," or to "heal them," according to James 5:15. He had faith to pray for healings, and he'd seen them happen in his ministry many times.

Up until the point this woman came with her request, however, Dad had never had an experience in his healing ministry where he had seen God do a creative miracle and put something into someone's body that had never been there before. But he had compassion for the mother and the boy, so he reached down and placed his hand on this young boy's right hip. It was flat.

When my father asked the woman why her son's hip was flat, she replied, "The doctors say he was born without a hip socket." This confirmed that she was asking for a creative miracle, not a healing.

Dad was honest with the woman, telling her, "I do not believe God will give us a creative miracle in this life. But I do believe that when Jesus comes again and the dead in Christ are resurrected, whatever was missing from our bodies in this life will be completely restored. At that time, your son will have a new body. So, in all honesty, I can't pray for your son because I don't believe God will give him a new hip socket."

Faith Is Where You Find It

Now, my father may not have had the faith at that time to pray and believe for a creative miracle. But that boy's situation wasn't dependent on Dad's faith. It was dependent on *someone* having faith. God looks for faith to respond to, wherever He can find it.

So, when the mother looked at my father with determination like he had never seen before, something began to happen in the spirit realm. The tears were flowing down her cheeks. But suddenly she rose up in her inner man, and she declared, "Oral Roberts, I don't ask you to believe for my son. All I ask is that you pray. *I'll* do the believing."

In telling this story over the years, Dad said that the mother's declaration didn't do much to move him to a place of faith. But the 10,000 people witnessing the whole exchange were very moved; a murmur ran through the crowd. Finally, Dad told everyone that because this mother had asked him to pray, he would do it. But he repeated that according to his understanding of God's Word, she was asking for a creative miracle, not a healing. He said, "I believe that will come in the resurrection."

During his healing crusades, my father usually asked people to lay their hands on the back of the chair in front of them as their point of contact to believe God for miracles while he prayed. This time, though, he didn't ask the audience to release their faith at all. He simply said a few words of prayer. But the people touched the chairs anyway. Dad said it felt like their prayers ascended to God like a powerful gust of wind. Then he finished praying for those in the healing line and went to his hotel to sleep.

The following day, Dad arrived at the tent for the next service in the crusade. One of his associates met him as soon as he got out of the car. "Do you remember the little boy without a hip socket that you prayed for last night?" the man asked.

Dad said, "Yes, what about him?"

Dad's associate was thrilled as he declared, "God has given him a new hip socket! We've had him walking back and forth on the platform without his crutches. He's running and jumping, just like any normal, perfectly healthy boy. The crowd has been crying and praising God the entire time."

My dad used to say you can never out-believe God. You can never believe for something that is beyond God's ability to do. The boy who was born without a hip socket is proof that God can perform a creative miracle.

But the boy's mother? That boy's mother is proof that if we have faith, we can receive whatever we ask for — just as Mark 11:22–24 tells us.

Nothing Is Too Hard for God

Miracles such as the one I've just told you about are not unusual. They're not rare. In God's way of doing and being, miracles are meant to happen in our lives whenever we believe God and allow Him to work in our circumstances. We see this in the ministry of Jesus when He walked the earth.

John 9 tells the story of a young man who was blind from birth. Verses 6-7 say that Jesus *spat on the ground and made clay with the saliva; and He anointed the eyes of the blind man with the clay. And He said to him, "Go, wash in the pool of Siloam"… So he went and washed, and came back seeing.*

Just as God took clay and molded Adam and breathed His life into him (Genesis 2:7), Jesus took clay, formed eyes for this man, and said, "Go, wash now." The man acted on what Jesus said, in faith. He went to the pool of Siloam and washed his eyes. And suddenly, he could see perfectly!

Mark 3:1-5 tells about a man who had a withered hand. Jesus spotted this man while He was in the synagogue on the Sabbath. He instructed the man to stretch out his hand, and as the man did so, his arm was restored!

John 11 tells of Lazarus, who had been dead for four days when Jesus arrived on the scene. Lazarus' body had been wrapped in long strips of cloth, which was the Jewish custom when burying a body. He was placed in a tomb, which was sealed shut with a stone. When Jesus ordered the people gathered around the tomb to remove the stone, Lazarus's sister Martha protested. "He's been dead four days," she said. "By now, he stinks" — meaning, "His body must be decomposing by now."

Jesus looked at Martha and said, "Did I not say to you that if you would believe, you would see the glory of God?" He lifted His head toward heaven and prayed, then He cried with a loud voice, *"Lazarus, come forth!"* And Lazarus walked out of that tomb, raised from the dead, grave clothes and all!

And these aren't all the miracles Jesus did. There are many others, so many others that the world isn't big enough to contain all the books that could be written about them (John 21:25).

You may ask, "Richard, what are you saying here?" I'm saying that I believe nothing is too difficult for God.

Friend, when Mark 11:22–24 tells us to ask God to meet *whatever* need we are facing, it means that there is nothing too hard for God to do. No circumstance, no situation, no diagnosis, no debt, no bad news will ever be so big, so overwhelming for God to handle.

When you feel your lack is too big for God to fill… when you feel your needs are too great and too complicated and too overwhelming for you to get on top of… when you feel your circumstances are so bad that there's no way for God to make a way for things to get better… when you feel your problems are out of control and can never be solved…

When you wonder if you're asking God to do something He can't do, remember that according to His Word, there's nothing too hard for God (Jeremiah 32:17; Luke 1:37). So, begin to believe and release your faith, not your doubt.

Expect God to honor His Word. Believe in confidence and faith that He keeps His promises. Know that He is not a liar, that He is true to His Word and He will do what He has said He will do. Stand in faith and come against your lack, in Jesus' Name.

Remember These Principles

- Your faith is what connects you to God's supply.

- Even when other people doubt, if you can believe for God to meet your needs, then you can get into a position to receive what you need from Him.

- There is nothing too hard, too difficult, or impossible for God.

SPEAK
THE WORD

CHAPTER SIX

Speaking the Word

Let me ask you a question. What's talking to you? Is it your circumstances, fear, worry, and doubt? Is it sickness, disease, financial problems, and family problems?

Our situations talk to us every day, trying to defeat us, trying to get us to give in to the work of the enemy in our lives and in the world around us. But we have authority in the name of Jesus to resist negative circumstances, emotions, and thoughts. Yes, all these things may talk to us. But as children of God, we have the Bible right to talk back, using God's Word and our faith to overcome.

God Formed the World with His Words

In Mark chapter 11, Jesus tells us to have faith in God. Another translation of that verse says, "Have the God-kind of faith." But what does it mean to have the God-kind of faith? What does that look like?

Well, we can see the God-kind of faith in action from the very beginning of the Bible. God used His kind of faith when He created the world.

Genesis 1:1–3

In the beginning God created the heavens and the earth. The earth was without form, and void; and darkness was on the face of the deep. And the Spirit of God was hovering over the face of the waters. Then God said, "Let there be light"; and there was light.

I want you to notice a few things in these verses. First of all, notice that it says *the earth was without form.* The earth was present, but it didn't have form. It was void and empty. Perhaps you could say it was like modeling clay or Play-Doh. It had volume and mass, but it didn't have shape. It lacked form.

The verse also says that *darkness was on the face of the deep.* Now, *darkness* means the absence of light. So, the world wasn't shaped. It wasn't orderly. It was dead and empty and dark. Does that remind you of some of the circumstances you are facing? Do areas of your life seem empty, dead or dying, or dark?

Let's look at what God did when faced with a similar situation. Genesis chapter 1 says He *created* the earth out of the formless, dead, empty situation He found it in. Like a sculptor takes clay and shapes it into something recognizable and functional, God took the earth and shaped it into the world we know and live in.

How did He do it? Genesis 1:3 gives us the answer — He said, "Let there be light." He spoke to the earth. He shaped it with His words.

God's Words Contain Power to Change a Situation

Now, when Genesis chapter 1 tells us that God spoke, the word used there is *ruach* — which can be translated as the wind of God, or the breath of God. It is the essence of who God is in action. It is the creative power and energy of God. And when He speaks it, His creative power and energy enters into the situation

He is speaking to.

When God spoke to the shapeless, dark, void earth, it means the creative *ruach* power of God came out of His mouth. And in the face of God's power, the earth had no choice but to obey. When God said, "Let there be light," the darkness had to obey, and light came forth. This is how God created every living thing in the world. He *spoke*, and existence obeyed Him.

Having the God-kind of faith, therefore, is having the same ruach power of God coming out of our mouth to address our lack and bring forth everything we have need of. And if we want that kind of power when we speak and pray, then it makes sense to use God's Word — because His Word contains the creative power to change things, just as we see in Genesis 1.

Talking to a Tree

Jesus understood what it meant to have the God-kind of faith. Not only did He tell us to operate with that kind of faith, but He showed us how to do it in His life and ministry. One of my favorite examples of how Jesus tapped into God's creative power with His words can be seen in Mark chapter 11.

Mark 11:12–14

When they had come out from Bethany, He was hungry. And seeing from afar a fig tree having leaves, He went to see if perhaps He would find something on it. When He came to it, He found nothing but leaves, for it was not the season for figs. In response Jesus said to it, "Let no one eat fruit from you ever again." And His disciples heard it.

Here, we see that Jesus was traveling with His disciples one day, and he was hungry. So, when He saw a fig tree bearing leaves, He immediately moved toward it. Clearly, He was expecting that a fig tree with leaves would also have fruit on it. But when He arrived at the foot of the tree, He saw clearly that it had no fruit on it. Jesus wanted to be fed, but there were no figs.

Many times in our lives, we find ourselves hungry for our needs to be met. Perhaps we hunger for healing, or forgiveness, or freedom from debt, or something else. But when we move toward what initially seems to be a good opportunity, we instead find ourselves with nothing. I believe the fig tree represents that type of situation in our lives.

When Jesus saw that the fig tree looked good but didn't have the fruit to meet His need, Mark 11:14 says something interesting. It says Jesus *responded* to the tree. Another version says He *answered* the tree. He said, "*Let no one eat fruit from you ever again.*"

Now, why do we answer something? We answer it because it was talking to us. That tree was talking! And what it was saying wasn't good. When the fig tree did not produce what it was supposed to, it was talking to Jesus. It was saying, "You created me, but I don't have to obey You. I don't have to bear fruit."

Jesus answered and said, "No one is ever going to eat from you again." Notice that He didn't pray, "Father God, let there be figs." He spoke directly to what the tree was saying. Why? Because when we face a situation that is causing us need or lack, we must speak to that situation and tell it what to do.

That's what God did when He saw the earth without form and void. He spoke directly to the darkness and told it to let there be light. He spoke to the earth and told it to produce fruit after its own kind. And when Jesus came across a fig tree which was not producing fruit after its own kind, He told it to dry up at the roots.

When we face a need, how are we to address it? Well, we don't need to tell God about it. He already knows the situation. He knows our hearts. And He knows what we need, even before we ask (Matthew 6:8). What we are to do is to speak directly to the need itself with God's Word. When we speak God's Word in faith to our situation, it brings the *ruach*, creative power of God into the situation to shape things for the better.

Don't Let Appearances Deceive You

Often, when we pray about a situation and speak to it by faith, we don't see immediate, visible changes. It often takes time for our circumstances to turn around for good. We experience a waiting period, but God is still at work behind the scenes to bring about a turnaround for us.

That's what happened with the fig tree. Jesus commanded it to never bear fruit again. In essence, He commanded it to die. But did it die immediately? No. From the outside, the tree looked exactly the same as it did when Jesus first approached it. To the natural eye, nothing happened.

Jesus walked away with the disciples, and they went about their business in Jerusalem. When they came back along the road a day later, they passed the fig tree. And that's when the disciples saw something that astounded them.

Mark 11:20–21

Now in the morning, as they passed by, they saw the fig tree dried up from the roots. And Peter, remembering, said to Him, "Rabbi, look! The fig tree which You cursed has withered away."

Notice that the fig tree was not just dead; it had dried up from the roots. Why is this significant? It's because the life-giving power of anything is in its roots. The life-giving power that causes a tree to grow is in the roots. You water the roots. If the roots dry up, the tree dries up. When you look at something that you're planting, if your flower is drying up on the outside, check the roots on the inside.

When the root of something is dried up, everything else has to follow, because the root is the source.

You may ask, "Why does this matter?" It matters because it explains why we must speak directly to our situation with God's Word if we want to see our situation change. Like Jesus and the fig tree, we are to speak to our circumstances and command them to change, in Jesus' Name. We are to tell sickness, "In Jesus' Name, I'm healed." We are to tell our financial situations, "My God shall supply all my need."

We must attack our lack with our faith, using God's Word to invite His creative power into the situation to turn it around for our good.

Tell Your Mountain to Move

When the disciples called Jesus' attention to the withered fig tree, He answered by saying:

"Have faith in God. For assuredly, I say to you, whoever says to this mountain, 'Be removed and be cast into the sea,' and does not doubt in his heart, but believes that those things he says will be done, he will have whatever he says. Therefore I say to you, whatever things you ask when you pray, believe that you receive them, and you will have them" (Mark 11:22-24).

This is where Jesus tells us to have the God-kind of faith. We are to use and operate in the same system of faith that God operates in. Remember, the kingdom of God has a specific way of operating. It is about seeking Him and putting Him first. It's about speaking in faith. It's about planting seed and expecting a harvest.

As we use the system of faith that God uses, we are to speak God's Word into our situation. We are to look at the mountain of need in our life and command it to change. We are to command it, by faith, to move out of our way. And if we'll say it in faith, and if we don't doubt in our heart but instead believe that there will be results, then what we say will come to pass.

Remember, God expected there to be light, and there was light. Jesus expected the fig tree to wither, and it withered. Likewise, we can expect our situations to change for the better when we speak God's Word in faith.

When should we believe that our situation is changing? We are to believe it *when we pray*. The moment you pray and speak God's Word, that's when you release your faith and begin expecting to see results. And like Jesus did with the fig tree, don't worry if you don't see immediate results. Go about your business, knowing that God's Word, spoken in faith, is at work bringing about a change that you will eventually see in the natural realm.

Remember These Principles

- God's Word is anointed, and it is full of creative power.

- When God wants a situation to change, He speaks to it in faith.

- We are to have the God-kind of faith — the kind of faith that speaks directly to the situation and expects a miracle.

- When we face circumstances that we desire to change, we are to speak directly to them, using God's Word to bring His creative power into our circumstances.

CHAPTER SEVEN

Say What God Says About Your Circumstances

To illustrate how important it is for us to use our faith in God's Word to walk in abundance and deliverance, my dad would tell the story of how his friend Charles Capps, a noted businessman and preacher, learned to live by faith and overcome his needs. I'll share it with you too, because I believe it will open up your eyes and show how God's Word can kickstart our faith and get God's miracle-working power into motion in our circumstances.

In the later years of his life, Charles Capps became a powerful preacher and teacher of God's Word. But he didn't start out that way. He started out as a poor farmer living in Arkansas, which was one of the poorest states in America at the time. And at first, he didn't know how to use his faith as a tool to attack the areas of lack in his life and turn things around.

Now, let me explain something...

Charles was a Christian, even in his younger years. He went to church faithfully, gave what he could into the offering, and hoped to make it to Heaven. He told my father that as a young man, he looked forward to going to Heaven. He thought it would be so much different from his life on earth, which was filled with discouragement, sickness, poverty, shame, doubt, and other troubles. He knew his needs would be met in Heaven. But he didn't know how he could use his faith here on earth for the things he needed before he got to Heaven.

On the inside, Charles had great potential. But no one could see it, not even himself. Then something happened that turned things around for him. But before that turnaround, he faced one of the worst times of his life.

His crops had failed. His bank loan was due. In the middle of what was already a crisis, he woke up one day to find himself sick in his body and in deep debt. Suddenly, he asked himself an important question: "Is this all there is to life? Is this all God has for me?"

As he searched for the answer to what God's plan was for his life, he did what any good Christian would do. He went to church. He read the Bible. He went to Sunday school. But it still seemed to him like his faith in God wasn't working to bring him relief. Even though he believed God's Word was true, he didn't know he could apply it in faith to his everyday challenges.

I know how it feels to face situations where it seems like my faith isn't working. You've probably felt that too, at times. Keep reading, and I'll share with you the revelation from God that turned around Charles' life.

Our Thinking Determines Our Believing

At this desperate time in his life, Charles told my father that he came across some biblical teaching that changed his way of approaching life. Among the teachings he discovered was a book by Kenneth E. Hagin, who was a friend of my father's and an anointed teacher when it came to applying faith to our lives. Through that book, called *Right and Wrong*

Thinking, Charles came to understand that he could use God's Word as a way to think, a way to believe, and a way to talk about his circumstances.

Before then, he had thought he just had to accept whatever circumstances came his way as the will of God. He thought if God wanted him to be sick, then he'd be sick, and there wasn't anything he could do about it. Likewise, he believed that if God wanted him well, then somehow he would be healed. But however it happened, it would be God doing all the work.

Charles didn't believe he had any power to do anything about his circumstances. He had become negative because he had fallen into believing and saying what other people said about God, instead of what God Himself said in His Word.

But as he studied what God was saying through the anointed teaching he was hearing on faith, he told my father, "I discovered I could be right with God in my heart but wrong in my head with my thinking. I realized when I thought wrong, I believed wrong, and when I believed wrong, I acted wrong in the practical matters of my life."

Do you realize the same can be true of any Christian — even you and me? It's possible to be saved and going to Heaven, yet still filled with all kinds of misconceptions about what God desires for us. And it's also possible, as Charles experienced, to be set free from our wrong thinking and see how our believing can turn our lives around.

Charles told my father that he began to see that he could pray according to God's Word and believe God to meet his needs. He realized that if he believed God's Word and did not doubt in his heart, he could have God's supply flowing into his life, filling his lack and meeting his needs, and thriving in God's abundance.

Are We Confessing God's Word, or the Devil's?

Any fish, even a dead one, can float downstream along with the current. But it takes a live fish to fight against the current and swim upstream. In the same way, we can easily go with the world's way of doing things. But it takes determination to focus on God's Word and go with His way of doing things.

That's what Charles Capps realized. "I began reading my Bible with an ear to what God said," he told my father. "Jesus had told us to let His sayings sink down deep into our hearts. I'd made the mistake of listening to what other people said. They really didn't know the Word of God themselves, and it was their opinion about God that I was listening to. So God's Word was not alive and moving in my heart or on my lips. I began to see that was where I had missed it."

Charles also reported having another major revelation one day while praying. He said that one day, while he was trying to pray, he just blurted out what he was thinking: "Lord, things are not working. Things are getting worse."

It had never occurred to him that God would speak to people today. So, he was shocked when he heard the Lord say something back to him in his spirit. He felt as if God was saying to him: "Who told you that?"

He stopped and thought a minute. Then he said, "Lord, it sure wasn't You. It must have been the devil."

He sensed the Lord saying to him in his inner man, "Yes, and I would appreciate it if you would quit telling Me what the devil said. You have been quoting the devil more than you have been quoting Me. You have been praying for Me to do something about your finances and about your physical body, but everything that comes out of your mouth is negative. It's the way the devil talks. If you don't change to believe My words and to say My words, your situation will not get better; it will get worse."

Charles decided he was ready to change the words that came out of his mouth. He asked the Lord what to do. The Lord told him, "Read and study My Word and find out what I said about it. Then start saying and praying the things I said about you instead of what the devil says."

Faith Comes by Hearing God's Word

It was like a million lights had come on in Charles' understanding when he heard God's Word in his spirit: *"Faith comes by hearing, and hearing by the Word of God."* That's when he realized that faith comes from whatever we hear. If we listen to what the devil is saying, we'll start to believe it. But if we'll hear and listen to God's Word, then His Word can begin to build faith in us for miracles according to His Word.

I encourage you to do what Charles Capps began to do — he searched the Word of God to find out what God said about him as a believer and made a list of it. He wrote down every scripture he found about God's promises to you and me as believers. He then began to confess them daily over his life. He carried his list of scriptures with him and confessed it while he was working.

He began to notice quickly when he fell back into negative talk, and he found it easier to correct his words and his prayers. He realized that in the past, he'd been praying about the problem, instead of praying God's solution. He had gotten into praying negative prayers, instead of the Word of God kind of prayers. This meant he had faith, but he was using it to believe he was not going to be able to meet his obligations. He had faith that he was going to fail even more than he was already failing.

But now, he was praying the solutions which he found in God's Word. Some days he carried his Bible to the fields with him.

While eating his lunch, he would find something the Scriptures said. Then he would pray, "Father, Your Word says, 'Whatsoever things I desire when I pray, believe that I receive them and I shall have them.' Therefore in the name of Jesus I pray, believing that my needs are met."

Don't Be Deterred by Roadblocks

Sometimes, as we are confessing God's Word, praying and believing for our needs to be met, we may find ourselves coming up against roadblocks. It may seem as though we are not moving forward. We're not seeing results. When this happens, it's important to be persistent in our faith and keep sowing our seeds.

That's what Charles Capps came to realize. He was facing a roadblock to his breakthrough. And then he discovered my father's book, *The Miracle of Seed-Faith*. In it, he found another important principle for tapping into the promises of God.

As a farmer, Charles already understood the natural laws of sowing and reaping God had set forth. He understood that he had to plant natural seeds in the soil in order to harvest a crop. But through my father's teaching, he came to see that the laws of sowing and reaping work in the spiritual realm too. Just as a farmer would plant seeds in good soil, then water them and care for them until the harvest came, we can plant our seeds of faith into God's kingdom, then pray over them and confess God's Word over them until we receive the answers to our prayers.

As we give, our faith becomes a seed that we release to God, expecting to reap a great harvest as the seed grows. Charles began to see that he could release his financial seed into the soil of God's kingdom. And according to Mark 10:29-30, he could expect a miraculous harvest — a hundredfold multiplication harvest of his seed *in this life*.

Give and It Shall Be Given to You

Luke 6:38 says, *Give, and it will be given to you: good measure, pressed down, shaken together, and running over will be put into your bosom. For with the same measure that you use, it will be measured back to you.*

Now, I've talked with many people over my years of ministry who have told me, "Richard, I give to the Lord. I tithe. I sow offerings. But I don't expect anything back." But Luke 6:38 tells us that we are to expect to receive something in return, because as we give, good things will be given back to us in good measure, pressed down, shaken together, and running over. When we get a revelation of this scripture deep down in our inner man, it does wonders to help us believe for and receive the harvests to meet our needs.

Charles told my father that when he realized he could begin *expecting a harvest* from his sowing, it revolutionized his prayer life. The words of Jesus in Luke 6:38 came alive to him. He began to pray, "Thank God because I have given, it is given to me. Lord, You said if I give, it shall be given to me. I don't have it now. I don't see it with my natural eyes. But as sure as You said it in Your Holy Word, it's already given. Now it's a matter of my receiving it. So I now look for and expect a miracle return to come to me."

Outwardly, he had nothing. His body was sick. He still faced a load of debts to the bank and others. He could see no light at the end of the tunnel. But he got hold of the Word of God concerning seed-faith, and it began to take root in him. He began to see himself as being prosperous, before he ever was prosperous in the natural. And because he saw and believed what God's Word said about him, in faith, believing, he began to regularly confess it too. The words of his mouth began to match God's Word.

And when the words of our mouth line up with God's Word,

and we are taking steps of faith and sowing our seed into God's kingdom, we can begin to expect and see harvests that will fill our lack to overflowing abundance.

If We Don't Give Up, Our Harvest Will Come

According to God's Word, we are to believe God and act in faith *before* we see the harvest. And we are to remain in faith, despite our circumstances. If we'll do this, then God can be at work in our lives, moving behind the scenes until the time is ripe for our harvest to come forth.

This is what Charles Capps experienced too. He had to persist in believing God and sowing seeds of his faith and confessing God's Word, even while things in his life looked desperate. But as he continued to do and say and believe what God said, faith continued to grow inside him. He was in a state of expectation as he held onto his confession of faith.

And then a breakthrough came. One day a woman called him and said, "Charles, we're going to sell our farm. Do you want to buy it?" Because he was firmly believing God for a harvest at this point, he was able to see this as an opportunity from God. He felt the Lord leading him to say yes. So, he agreed to buy the land.

When he hung up the phone, his wife asked where he was going to get the money to pay for the farm. He said, "Money is no problem."

Can you picture that? This man who had previously been in doubt about his future, who had been so negative about his prospects, was now able to believe God by faith for what he needed — which in this case was the money to pay for the land. He was believing in his heart that the seed he had sown to God in tithes, offerings, and prayers was bringing him his harvest, according to Mark 11:22–24 and Luke 6:38.

When Charles went to close the deal, they didn't ask for any money down—not one dollar. Then an opportunity came for him to sell 40 acres of the land he had just purchased to the school district to build a new school on, and he took it. When the title deed came to him, he had $57,000 equity in the farm — and he hadn't paid a dime for it.

Now, I want you to keep in mind that Charles was not operating on presumption. He had a specific word from God about the property, so he planted his seed and attached his faith to it. He listened to the voice of the Holy Spirit to step out and purchase the property. Because he obeyed God, in faith, God brought forth a miracle for him.

We Are Blessed

In his later years, as he ministered on what he had learned, Charles Capps' favorite saying became, "I am blessed." When asked what he meant by that, he would say:

"When I saw what God was saying to me in His Word and I began to believe and confess it and to call it into my life, in less than one year I'd broken the devil's supernatural hold over me.

"People began asking me to share my testimony. I didn't know I could talk in public. I'd had such a poor image of myself, it scared me to death to open my mouth about God to somebody else. But the more people asked me, the more I opened up.

"Pretty soon, some said I was talking like Oral Roberts. I said, 'That's OK. Oral talks like God talks. God talks seedtime and harvest, and Oral talks it. God talks healing for our souls, our bodies, our minds and our finances. Oral talks it. God has used Oral, and I want Him to use me.'

"I was excited about God and wanted others to get excited about Him too. Pretty soon, about half of my friends had Oral's book *The Miracle of Seed-Faith*. We turned into a community of seed-faith believers. God our source began to meet our needs, to make us prosperous, happy Christians. And we began thriving in God's abundance!"

As Charles learned to expect a miracle to meet his needs, it changed the way he felt about God and the way he felt about himself. He began to see himself healed and prosperous. He began to see himself as a victorious, overcoming child of God, no matter what his circumstances looked like at the time.

This is one reason my father always loved teaching about seed-faith, and so do I. When God's people meditate on God's Word, get it down into their spirit, and confess His Word in faith, they can begin to change how they see themselves and their situation. They can begin to see that no matter how bad their current circumstances may seem, things can change for the better. Our situation can turn around for our good, if we will just continue to believe God, sow our seeds, and expect a harvest.

What Are You Confessing Today?

What I hope you have caught as you read Charles Capps' story is that our thinking, our believing, and our speaking are so important to determining what we receive in life. If we want to change what we are receiving, if we want to change our circumstances, then we must begin to pay attention to what we are saying, thinking, and believing.

So today, I encourage you to listen to yourself. Listen to your own words. Listen to how you pray. Are you saying what the devil says? Are you saying you're not going to make it? Are you talking about how sick and in debt and desperate you are? Are you confessing the problem, instead of confessing God's solution for the problem?

Or, are you speaking God's Word in faith over your life? Are you coming against the areas of need and lack in your life by using God's Word? Are you talking about God's provision, His promises, His blessings? Are you confessing that you are receiving His supply for your lack?

If you're not confessing what God says about you and your situation, then it's time to change your confession! Remember the words of King David in Psalm 19:14: *Let the words of my mouth and the meditation of my heart be acceptable in Your sight, O Lord, my strength and my Redeemer.* As you choose to meditate on God's Word, get it into your heart, and speak it with your mouth, you are opening up ways for God to move in your life to meet your needs and to thrive in His abundance.

Remember These Principles

- It takes determination to focus on God's Word and go with His way of doing things, especially when our circumstances look bad.

- We will never change our situation by continuing to speak negatively about it.

- When we believe God's Word and speak it in faith, continually, over our lives, God will begin to move in our circumstances to do miracles.

CHAPTER EIGHT

When We Think We're Out of Options, the Word of God Says We're Not

Have you ever felt as though you are totally out of options and have nowhere else to go? If you've ever felt like you've been backed into a corner—or maybe you feel that way now—well then, I have a word of encouragement. God can still turn your situation around, even now. You are not without hope.

How do I know this? Well, the Bible is filled with examples of situations that looked impossible to overcome, yet God made a way for His people where there seemed to be no way. Let's look at one of them... the life of Samson, which is found in Judges 14–16. I encourage you to read it for yourself.

Now, Samson was a man who seemed to have everything going for him. Then he disobeyed God, lost his power, and got into bondage so deep that it seemed he would never have a way out. But in the end, God made a way for him.

Samson was called by God to deliver God's people, the children of Israel, from the oppression of the Philistines, who ruled over them at the time. When the Spirit of God came upon Samson, his body became supernaturally strong, and he was able to defeat large numbers of Philistines.

On one occasion, he was trapped inside one of their fortified cities. They planned to kill him. His only way out was through the city gate, which was closed and barred. Feeling the Spirit of God come upon him, Samson took hold of the heavy gate, ripped it out, and carried it off on his shoulders.

Another time, a thousand soldiers of the Philistines attacked him. He was unarmed and alone, but he picked up the jawbone of a dead donkey and used it as a weapon. When the battle was over, Samson was alive and well. The enemy soldiers — one thousand of them — lay dead. The word went forth throughout the land — "Samson is a mighty deliverer!"

Know Who Your Source Is

But as amazing as Samson's mighty feats were, they were not of his own doing. He was not the source of his own strength. God was His source. When he depended on the anointing of God to empower him, he could do great and mighty things. But when he disobeyed God and relied on his own strength, Samson became like any other man. This became a harsh reality to him when he became careless and thought he could handle things by himself.

The Philistines found a beautiful, cunning woman named Delilah and paid her to spend time with Samson and discover the secret of his power. Delilah seduced Samson. And as a result, Samson got his mind off God and his calling as a deliverer of God's people. He thought he could handle anything, including her, without God's strength behind him.

Eventually, he revealed to Delilah that the source of his strength and success was a vow he had made to serve God. That vow was symbolized by seven locks of long hair, which he had vowed never to cut. That night, as Samson lay asleep in Delilah's arms, she cut off his hair. Then she wakened him and told him the Philistines were there to attack him. He went out to face them, believing that he would defeat them just as he always had. He didn't know that his strength — the anointing of God — had left him.

For the first time in his life, Samson suffered a terrible, agonizing defeat. The Philistines bound him, gouged out his eyes, and tied him up in the place of a mule to grind at the mill of their god, Dagon. Around and around he went, grinding at the mill day after day, blind, defeated, his God-given strength gone. Everything he had was gone. Even God, it seemed, was gone. It seemed like there was no way out for him anymore.

But the Bible says *the hair of his head began to grow again after it had been shaven* (Judges 16:22). I imagine he must have been amazed the day he felt his hair growing back. Perhaps he felt it tickling the back of his neck one day, while he was chained at the mill, laboring hard. And reaching back, he felt it — his hair was returning. And with it, maybe his strength would return too.

I believe Samson began to have hope then that there was a way out of his seemingly impossible defeat. He began to believe again. And in that moment, as he felt the Spirit of God stirring inside him, he prayed to God for a second chance. I believe that in that moment, Samson realized he had not fully appreciated God's calling on his life. And so, he made a new decision to obey God. The moment he sensed God's presence again, he made a decision that he would not fail God again.

The Key Is Obedience

So, Samson believed God and waited for a change in his situation. And all the while, his hair was growing back. Then one day, the lords of the Philistines were meeting in the temple of their god, celebrating their victory over Israel and the imprisonment of God's deliverer, Samson, in their midst. They called for Samson so they could entertain themselves at his expense.

As Samson entered the temple, packed with the lords and ladies of the Philistines, a cheer went up to their god, Dagon. They amused themselves by laughing at Samson, who was blind and seemingly defenseless. Eventually, Samson had an opportunity to do something to turn things around. He asked for permission to rest against the pillars in the center of the temple, where he was on display as a laughingstock.

Standing now between the two pillars that supported the entire temple, renewed in his commitment to God and sensing the Spirit of God's presence again in his life, Samson realized he had a new option, a way out where there had been no way before.

Judges 16:28–30

Then Samson called to the Lord, saying, "O Lord God, remember me, I pray! Strengthen me, I pray, just this once, O God, that I may with one blow take vengeance on the Philistines for my two eyes!"

And Samson took hold of the two middle pillars which supported the temple, and he braced himself against them, one on his right and the other on his left.

Then Samson said, "Let me die with the Philistines!" And he pushed with all his might, and the temple fell on the lords and all the people who were in it. So the dead that he killed at his death were more than he had killed in his life.

Never Give Up!

The Bible declares that we *should always pray and not give up* (Luke 18:1 NIV). It's so easy to give up, tell ourselves it's all over, and let the devil have his way rather than God have His way. It's so tempting to give in to the feeling that we are not worth anything to anyone, and that no one cares. It's easy to look at negative circumstances and think that things look so bad, there's no hope for you… that you're out of options and even God can't help.

But prayer still changes things.

Samson could have given up for good. He could have thought, "Sure, I once carried off the gate of a city and killed a thousand Philistine soldiers with nothing but the jawbone of a donkey, but I'm too weak and defeated to pull this temple down on the heads of the enemies of the Lord God of Israel. I've failed the Lord and myself, so I'm out of options."

He could have decided to just accept his imprisonment. He could have refused to make a move in faith because it seemed unlikely that he could push against the pillars hard enough to cause the temple roof to collapse.

Instead of giving up, Samson prayed to God one more time. He asked God to remember him in spite of his failures and mistakes. He asked to have the Spirit of the Lord flow through his arms one more time. And as he pushed the pillars, they began to move. The building shook. The temple collapsed. And the Philistines were crushed… All because God made a way for Samson where there had seemed to be no way.

God Can Make a Way for You Too

God is no respecter of persons (Acts 10:34). What He did for Samson, He can also do for you and me. Samson was no different from anyone. He was a man who committed himself to God, and we can do the same. The Spirit of God flowed through him, and God can work through us too. He trusted God, and so can we.

No matter what you may be facing right now, never forget that there is still hope. God isn't out of options. God can never be backed into a corner that He can't get out of. Remember this:

The Red Sea couldn't stop God. (See Exodus 14.)

The fiery furnace couldn't destroy Him. (See Daniel 3.)

The prophets of Baal couldn't stop Him. (See 1 Kings 18.)

Enemy kings couldn't kill Him. (See Matthew 2.)

The grave couldn't hold Him! (See John 20.)

And because we are in Christ, we have access to His ability to overcome all things. He can do miraculous works through us, if we will believe it and allow Him to work in and through our lives. We can do all things through Christ who strengthens us (Philippians 4:13).

With God, we are never out of options! It's not over for God's people. There is always a new beginning we can step into as we choose to believe Him and take a stand in faith.

Remember These Principles

- God can turn your situation around. You are not without hope.
- When Samson decided to believe God again, he began to find a way out of his seemingly impossible situation.
- It's easy to focus on negative circumstances, but God can turn things around for us.
- Prayer changes things. So, don't give up on your prayers, even if it takes time for the answer to come.
- There is always an opportunity for a new beginning when we believe God and take a stand in faith.

SOWING

CHAPTER NINE

You Can Attack Your Lack with Your Giving

During his life, my dad often shared the story of how he grew up sick and poor in Oklahoma. He would tell what it was like dreaming of someday getting out of poverty. Here, in his own words, is what he said about his childhood struggles:

"Papa was a preacher. I grew up in church and under the preaching of the Word of God. But I dreamed of being a lawyer and walking in the footsteps of my grandfather and hero, Amos Pleasant Roberts, who had been a judge in Indian Territory in Oklahoma where I was born and raised. That dream was so big in me, I couldn't care less about getting saved. In fact, I falsely believed if I got saved, that would mean I would never get to go to law school, become a lawyer, and later fulfill my highest dream of someday becoming governor of Oklahoma.

"Three events changed my mind. First, at age 17 I was struck down with tuberculosis. In that day, I had no hope of a medical cure. Second, people in the church who didn't believe in healing came to me and nearly turned me away from God forever. Third, Papa believed I was going to die and, wanting me to get saved so I would go to Heaven when that happened, he said, 'Oral, I'm going to kneel here and pray for you to be saved tonight. I will not get off my knees until you give your heart to God.'

"As I listened to my father's prayers to get saved, I felt nothing. I felt no desire at all to repent of my sins and ask God to save my soul. I had never felt any feelings that I wanted to be saved. But as Papa raised up on his knees and lifted his voice so that I could look right down over my body to the end of the bed and see his face, I had a vision. Suddenly Papa's face faded, and I saw the countenance of Jesus.

"In that instant, everything inside me broke loose. Seeing Jesus, I wanted salvation. I heard myself say, 'Jesus! Jesus! Save me!' My conversion was powerful, and God got hold of my life forever. Instantly I knew I was not to be a lawyer, but a preacher of the Gospel!"

The Greatest Gift

You may ask, "Richard, what does your father's salvation have to do with giving and receiving and my thriving in God's abundance? What does it have to do with figuring out how I can get my own needs met?"

Friend, it has everything to do with it! You see, Jesus is the greatest gift God the Father has ever given. My father saw Jesus as the greatest gift God gave him, and Jesus is the greatest gift God has ever given me. Jesus is the greatest gift God has given to everyone who will believe and receive Him.

Because we have accepted His gift of Jesus, we are part of the harvest that God has received back from His giving. That is an awesome eye-opener on what it means to give and receive back. It means that all God has is a result of what He has given.

Everything we have... our life, our work, our calling... it all belongs to God now because we have given our lives to Him. And everything He has — abundance, healing, forgiveness, deliverance, comfort, joy, peace, wisdom, and provision for our daily needs in life — all of this belongs to us, through Christ, because we have accepted Him into our hearts.

When God Had a Need, He Gave First

Can God have a need? The Bible tells us He did. He had a need to save us.

Remember, when Adam sinned in the Garden of Eden and fell from his sinless relationship with God, all his descendants fell too. Both spiritually and physically, all of humanity — including you and me — were lost. We were all separated from the God who created us. God lost us all!

God loved us, and yet He was separated from us and we were separated from Him because of sin. Man, whom He had created and to whom He had given His own nature, defied God, turned from Him, and went his own way. And Man, in his own power, could not save himself.

God had one option available to Him. He could *give*. He could offer someone to pay the price for sin in the place of Man, who could not pay the price. And He didn't choose an angel to do it. He chose to give Jesus, His only begotten Son, for our sake.

And here's the interesting thing — God gave Jesus to get something back! He didn't give just to give. He didn't give, expecting nothing in return. He gave with a clear, firm expectation of a harvest. He was planting a seed, so He could reap the miracle of my salvation, your salvation, and the salvation of any person who accepts Jesus as Lord.

God so loved us that He gave Jesus, in full expectation that He would receive back the thing He desired most: to redeem us back from the kingdom of darkness. He gave one Son, and He received back many sons and daughters over the centuries as people have given their lives to Christ and become born again. He gave His love and got back our love. He gave, and He received back from His giving.

God gave to get a return. And He received a harvest from what He gave, in faith, believing. Hebrews 12:2 says that Jesus endured the shame and death of the cross for *the joy that was set before Him.* The joy was the harvest! The joy was our salvation and restoration back to God!

And just as God gave and received back a harvest from His giving, you and I can give, in faith, with the expectation that we will receive a return on what we give. What we sow produces a harvest that comes back to us. As we continue to plant seeds to God in faith, believing, we can continue to receive harvests from our sowing.

And we, too, can experience the joy that comes from receiving the harvest that meets our needs!

Your Lack Can Be Filled

At times, our needs can seem so great that it's hard to imagine them ever being met. But through God, any lack we're facing can be overcome. We *can* prosper; we can thrive. We *can* find fulfillment and joy in this life. It's possible to experience a full, abundant life in which our needs are met.

And don't forget Luke 6:38, which tells us we can expect our giving to turn into receiving. You see, as we begin to receive the things that God has for us... the jobs, the debts paid, the healings, the restoring of relationships... these things begin to meet our needs and fill our lack. We can begin to have a life filled with miracles...blessings...goodness...and everything else God has for us.

My dad learned that as he sowed seeds in faith, expecting to receive a harvest to meet his needs, then and only then would his needs be met. And he taught this to me. And then I had to act on it in faith, believing that as I sowed my seeds, I would also receive a harvest. And I, too, discovered this great biblical truth that if I gave first, God would bless it back to me good measure, pressed down, shaken together, and running over.

Just as it took an act of God's love and faith for Him to give His only Son for us, it took His love and faith for Him to receive the harvest — our salvation. And just as we give in faith, we can receive back in faith. And as we do this continually in our lives, sowing against our needs, we can receive answers and have our needs met.

Remember, your harvest begins with the sowing of your seed. And it takes faith both to sow it and to expect to reap from it. Your seed and your faith are inseparably linked together to attack your lack and bring about your victory.

Remember These Principles

- When God faced a need to restore fallen humanity, He sowed a seed toward His need. He sowed Jesus.

- God gave first, and then He received a harvest.

- Just as God gave first, we also are to sow first, and then expect that seed to produce the harvest that meets our needs.

- Your seed and your faith are linked together. You must sow in faith and expect in faith for the seed to yield a harvest.

CHAPTER TEN

On Reaping Your Harvest, God Says, "Give It Time!" and "Don't Give Up!"

My dad would often tell the story of how growing up on a farm taught him what it takes for a seed to grow. One of the most interesting stories he would tell was not about the planting time or the harvest time, but about the growing time in between. He felt like the growing time could cause frustration and discouragement if it seemed unproductive.

I'd like to share what Dad had to say about this in his own words. Dad said:

> "I remember how Papa had to teach me about the growing time of a seed. After we planted, I'd run out the next day or two to see if the radishes or onions or tomatoes were already up. I'd rush out to the fields to see if the cotton or corn or wheat had grown enough to be ready to harvest.

> "As a child, I was unaware of God's laws of growth for the seed. Papa would say, 'Oral, give it time! Give it time!'

"As I grew older and became more experienced in planting seed with Papa and my brother Vaden, I began to understand there is a growing time that comes between seedtime and harvest time. During the growing time, we would water the seed when the rains didn't come. Then we would hoe around the young plant to remove the weeds from hindering its growth. We tended the plant to give it the best chance possible to grow and mature."

There Is a Growing Time for Our Seeds to Become Miracles

Dad went on to say:

"As a preacher's son, I grew up understanding tithing. When I became a Christian, the first thing I did was to start tithing, or giving the first tenth of my earnings to the Lord's work. As I did, I reverted to my childhood and expected God's miracle return to come overnight. It didn't occur to me there is a growing time in the spiritual laws of seedtime and harvest, just as there is in the natural realm.

"Worse still, I had no one to teach me, 'Oral, give it time! Give it time!' When the return didn't come quickly, I fell into a self-defeating habit of not expecting anything ever to come back from God from the tithes and offerings I was planting into His kingdom. It was as if I'd planted corn and didn't find a crop the next day, so I just wandered off.

"No one I knew in the church, including the pastors and evangelists I fellowshipped with, taught that our tithes and offerings were seeds we sowed.

We didn't have any perspective that if we sowed our giving, God would grow it and we would reap from it. Therefore, we didn't think about the increase or harvest time coming to us from the seed we planted.

"The preachers I listened to made reference to paying tithes and offerings. They didn't seem to understand prospering because it was the tradition of the church to associate 'poor' with 'humble' — as if poverty and humility were the same word. Even though prosperity was found throughout the Bible, it was not a teaching I had ever heard from the pulpit. So concerning offerings, the emphasis was on paying tithes rather than giving being balanced with receiving back from God.

"As a result, I made the mistake of becoming great in my giving, faithful to the point of sacrifice, but poor in my receiving. In our family, including my preacher papa, we felt we ought to pay our tithes and offerings, but we had no knowledge that we were supposed to expect the increase and reap the harvest that God inevitably gives to those who give to Him. Often, it became a burden to pay the first tenth of what we earned — and we were earning precious little. We had no scriptural concept that our earnings were meant to increase through regular harvest times, which God had promised us.

"Therefore, we grew poorer and poorer. In the natural, we were ten percent poorer with each dollar we gave, when all the time we could have been increasing our incomes had we known we were supposed to reap a harvest from the seed we sowed. This was one of the reasons that we gradually were drawn into Satan's net of false believing that if we became a Christian, we were supposed to be poor."

Poverty Is Not a Blessing

Dad also said:

"Certainly, if poverty were a blessing, my own family would have been considered blessed beyond measure because we were extremely poor. But I discovered that being hungry, having little to no provision, and watching Mama and Papa struggle to feed their family was not a blessing from God in any way whatsoever. I learned that it's not poverty that saves, but faith in the shed blood of Jesus and His resurrection from the dead. It's not poverty that meets our needs on our way to Heaven. It's our seed-faith of planting, giving as an offering of our seeds first, then reaping our harvests which is God's absolute promise to us."

Dad believed — and so do I — that as Christians, we can't successfully come against the lack and need in our lives and thrive if we are laboring under the bondage of believing we have to 'pay' God our tithes and offerings. Why? Because we can never pay. We can never pay God enough to make up for our sins. For that reason, God sent His Son to the Cross, and there He paid the debt for us. Therefore, our giving is not a debt we owe, but a seed we sow.

Dad liked to use tithes and offerings as an example because he used to think of giving as only relating to money. And there is some truth to that statement. Our money is part of us. It represents our time, our energy, our work, our talents, and our skills. It is the medium of exchange for what we need. And so we can give it to God's work, and we can receive a harvest from our giving.

But what's true for giving tithes and offerings is true for other types of giving and receiving as well. We can't pay God for loving us by just loving someone on this earth. We can't pay God for sending Jesus to this earth by spending time in volunteer service. We can't pay God by being good or doing the right things. All these acts are valuable, of course. They help us and they help others. But we can never pay God back for what He gives us through our own actions. It's impossible.

The Bible is very clear on this point. It isn't our good works that save us, but our faith in Jesus Christ (Ephesians 2:8–9). We can't pay God off. We can't pay God back. We can't pay to receive a miracle. We can't pay God at all.

But what we can do is give to Him as a seed we sow, in faith, believing that He has more than enough supply for us. Then, we can expect, by faith, that God's law of seedtime and harvest is going into effect to meet our needs. This is His law, His system, for meeting us at the point of our need and addressing our lack with His abundance. He produces harvests from the seeds we sow.

Why Do We Give Then?

I want to share with you some additional insights my dad had into our giving, because I believe it will build your faith to sow and expect a miraculous supply for your needs. Again, I'm using his words here because they are so powerful.

Dad said:

"As a little boy helping plant seeds, I remember the excitement we all felt about what we were going to get back when harvest time came. It didn't take long for me to see that the harvests that came in late summer or fall were hundreds of times greater than the small number of seeds we had planted the previous spring. From a few pounds of seed, we got much more produce as a harvest.

"Planting time was joyous because we thought of harvest time. And when we had picked our cotton, my brother Vaden and I would go with Papa to the cotton gin in town to sell it. We knew Papa would get money to buy the things we needed, including giving us some money to buy candy and soda pop! It turned the work into an exciting expectation of receiving better things for the entire family.

"I must admit I didn't get that excitement in church when the pastor said, 'Now everyone, pay your tithes and offerings this morning to the Lord,' for he didn't say anything at all about God opening the windows of Heaven and pouring blessings directly upon us, or that God would rebuke the devourer for our sake because we had honored Him with the first fruits of our increase.

Malachi 3:10–11 (KJV)

Bring ye all the tithes into the storehouse, that there may be meat in mine house, and prove me now herewith, saith the Lord of hosts, if I will not open you the windows of heaven, and pour you out a blessing, that there shall not be room enough to receive it. And I will rebuke the devourer for your sakes, and he shall not destroy the fruits of your ground; neither shall your vine cast her fruit before the time in the field, saith the Lord of hosts.

"This grew into a spirit of poverty that brought me into bondage as far as prospering as God's child was concerned. I know one thing — it took a lot of the joy out of serving the Lord for me. It was more than 12 years after I became a tither that I first began to learn to accept the Cross as 'paid in full' for all I owed. Then I could give as a seed I sowed and, from it, expect God to give me His rich harvests back in the form of my need. That's when my walk with Christ took on the excitement that continues to grow as I learn better how to live in seed-faith day after day.

"Why do I give? I give seeds so that I might receive a harvest. My time. My money. My acts of kindness. My smiles and encouraging words. They are *seeds*. They are compacted bundles of miracles that can burst forth. They are *harvest-producing* gifts unto God.

Seed Grows Invisibly

"One important thing I learned as a child was that the seed we planted grew invisibly. As a very young child, I thought when we put the seed in the ground and covered it up with the dirt, it disappeared! It was gone and we had nothing to show for our labor.

"What I didn't know was that God's Word teaches that everything visible came from something invisible (Hebrews 11:3).

"I'd rush around pestering Papa about where the seed went. He'd say, 'It's growing.'

'Papa, how do you know?'

"He'd shake his head and say, 'Just wait and you'll see.'

"As a Christian I spent the first 12 years paying

all my tithes and offerings, never missing once, not realizing that my seeds were growing all the time. When my tithes and offerings left my hands, I couldn't see them anymore. I didn't know that, like the natural seeds I'd planted, they were now in the good soil of the Gospel. Just as my physical eyes couldn't see the seed growing under the soil, I was not seeing my tithes and offerings growing.

"Neither did I know the methods to apply for cultivating my seed in the spiritual realm. I had learned what it meant to irrigate, cultivate, weed, and so forth in the natural — but not in the spiritual! I had to learn how to tend the soil I planted in, to keep my eyes on God who would multiply what I had sown. I had to speak faith talk instead of doubt talk, to weed out of my mind my impatience, my doubt, my worry, and my feelings that I was to give but not receive back a harvest."

They're Growing Good

"Papa would wait until our seeds began to sprout and push their way up as plants through the earth so we could see them. Then he'd say to Vaden and me, 'Come on, boys. Let's go see how big the plants are.'

"I remember he'd stand there and study the field with those little shoots coming up out of the ground. He would stoop down and feel them to see how healthy they were. Then he would say, 'Let's go back to the house. They're growing good.' It was such a great feeling.

"It took me many years to throw off the old

teaching, or lack of teaching, that I was to give but not expect anything back. When I finally began to get my breakthrough, I saw that God Himself is the 'good soil' — the soil I can't see but which is eternal and ever abundant and faithful in reproducing my seed sown into harvests for me to receive.

"I began to lose that old feeling that when my tithes and offerings left my hand, they were gone, just gone. I gained an excitement that those seeds were being placed in God's hands, and He would see that not one of my seeds would fail to grow or multiply. I couldn't see it in the natural, but I could know it because I saw it in God's Word, and I knew His Word could never fail me."

A Personal Harvest Too

"A third thing emerged from my childhood experience in planting seed and being part of the harvest time. I came to know that the harvest wasn't just good for my family and others in our town. It was good for me, personally, individually.

"As a Christian, there were many times I gave without believing that God would not only use my giving for the Gospel's sake but also use my giving for my sake. I gave, believing God would use my gift out there somewhere, for someone, to meet some need. But I never thought about it meeting my need or coming back in a harvest that would touch my life.

"That spirit was exactly opposite to the way I felt about our seeding and harvesting in the natural. What happened to the harvest in the natural? It helped the entire family. We paid the rent... the utilities... put gas in the car. We were able to buy necessities.

"The harvest also helped me, Oral, the youngest son. I got new shoes. I got clothes. I even got that soda pop and bit of candy now and then. And when we bought those things, that helped other people in our town. They could eat and use part of our harvest.

"The harvest helped me, and it helped others. It was a dual harvest. The same is true for a spiritual harvest. Your giving creates a harvest for you, and it creates a harvest for others."

The Double-Release

"When I saw that dual harvest, I began to get into the habit of a double-release. First, I released my tithes and offerings as seed. Second, I released my faith to God, believing He would multiply my seed sown into harvests for others and for me to receive back for my needs. I wrapped my seed with my faith. That's why I began to call it seed-faith.

"How happy I've been in my giving ever since! I know now that receiving follows my giving. I will have joy in receiving, not only in my giving, but in my receiving."

How the Harvest Comes

"I remember when I discovered Jesus' words in Luke 6:38.

Luke 6:38 (AMPC)

Give, and [gifts] will be given to you; good measure, pressed down, shaken together, and running over, will they pour into [the pouch formed by] the bosom [of your robe and used as a bag]. For with the measure you deal out [with the measure you use when you confer benefits on others], it will be measured back to you.

"As a Christian beginning to understand the laws of sowing and reaping, I began to see that God wasn't going to rain money down from Heaven, nor would He rain down clothes or cars or houses or lands or food or any other material thing we needed. That comes from men and women — human beings — who control portions of God's earth. It is people who are the instruments that God our source works through.

"It was so simple once I saw it. It was so powerful once I put it into practice as a way of life for my giving and receiving."

What to Do While We Wait for the Harvest

I trust that my father's story about learning the principles of seed-faith, in his own words, has inspired you to sow your seeds and believe for harvests. I know it has inspired Lindsay and me over the years.

It's a miracle for a seed sown to burst forth through the soil and become plants that produce fruit that grow into a mighty harvest. But it's a miracle that doesn't just happen. It must be made to happen. There are steps involved — from preparing the soil and sowing the seed, to watering everything and fertilizing and weeding until the harvest comes.

Receiving our harvests from God requires us to take steps too — steps of faith. As we can see from what Dad said — and from stories like the one belonging to Charles Capps in chapter 7 — receiving a harvest from our seed sown takes faith. After we sow our seed, we must tend it.

How do we do that? How do we 'tend' a seed of our time, our finances, our kindness, and anything else we have given to God in faith? For starters, we can 'water' our seed with our words. We can confess God's Word over the seed we sow as we await our harvest time.

What do I confess as I sow my seeds to God and wait for my harvests?

I confess with my mouth that I have given to God my tithes and offerings of every dollar I've earned to date, and they are in God's hands as seeds of my faith.

I confess with my mouth that my seed has been sown in the good soil of God's kingdom, and God is growing it invisibly, but absolutely.

I confess with my mouth that God is changing my seedtime into harvest time.

I confess with my mouth that God is rebuking the devourer for my sake.

I confess with my mouth that my giving is causing the windows of heaven to open up on my behalf.

I confess that God is pouring out ideas and insights into my mind about what to do and how to experience miracles greater than I can imagine in my life.

What does it mean when I say I "confess with my mouth" these things? I mean that I actually say these words out loud as I pray, worship God, and encourage myself in the Lord. I don't just think them. I say them. I say them continually.

I also like to confess out loud the scriptures that say God is at work on my behalf to bring about a harvest on my sowing:

Luke 6:38 — *Give, and it will be given to you: good measure, pressed down, shaken together, and running over will be put into your bosom. For with the same measure that you use, it will be measured back to you.*

Malachi 3:10–11 — *"Bring all the tithes into the storehouse, that there may be food in My house, and try Me now in this," says the Lord of hosts, "if I will not open for you the windows of heaven and pour out for you such blessing that there will not be room enough to receive it. And I will rebuke the devourer for your sakes, so that he will not destroy the fruit of your ground, nor shall the vine fail to bear fruit for you in the field," says the Lord of hosts.*

3 John 2 — *Beloved, I pray that you may prosper in all things and be in health, just as your soul prospers.*

John 10:10 — *The thief does not come except to steal, and to kill, and to destroy. I have come that they may have life, and that they may have it more abundantly.*

Isaiah 55:10–11 — *For as the rain comes down, and the snow from heaven, and do not return there, but water the earth, and make it bring forth and bud, that it may give seed to the sower and bread to the eater, so shall My word be that goes forth from My mouth; it shall not return to Me void, but it shall accomplish what I please, and it shall prosper in the thing for which I sent it.*

2 Corinthians 9:8 — *And God is able to make all grace abound toward you, that you, always having all sufficiency in all things, may have an abundance for every good work.*

I encourage you to memorize these verses. Write them down

and keep them where you can look at them often. And speak them out loud daily as you believe God for miracles.

Remember These Principles

- Our seeds take time to grow into a harvest. We must give it time.

- Our giving to God is not a debt we owe, but a seed we sow.

- Just as we sow natural seeds and expect a natural harvest, we are to give to God, expecting a harvest from Him to meet our needs.

- As we wait for our seeds of faith to grow, we can tend them and position ourselves for our harvest by continually confessing the Word of God.

CHAPTER ELEVEN

Can I Ask, "What's in It for Me?"

One day, a prosperous young man came to Jesus. He asked Jesus to give him life — real life.

Mark 10:17–27

Now as He was going out on the road, one came running, knelt before Him, and asked Him, "Good Teacher, what shall I do that I may inherit eternal life?"

So Jesus said to him, "Why do you call Me good? No one is good but One, that is, God.

You know the commandments: 'Do not commit adultery,' 'Do not murder,' 'Do not steal,' 'Do not bear false witness,' 'Do not defraud,' 'Honor your father and your mother.'"

And he answered and said to Him, "Teacher, all these things I have kept from my youth."

Then Jesus, looking at him, loved him, and said to him, "One thing you lack: Go your way, sell whatever you have and give to the poor, and you will have treasure in heaven; and come, take up the cross, and follow Me."

But he was sad at this word, and went away sorrowful, for he had great possessions.

Then Jesus looked around and said to His disciples, "How hard it is for those who have riches to enter the kingdom of God!"

And the disciples were astonished at His words. But Jesus answered again and said to them, "Children, how hard it is for those who trust in riches to enter the kingdom of God!

It is easier for a camel to go through the eye of a needle than for a rich man to enter the kingdom of God."

And they were greatly astonished, saying among themselves, "Who then can be saved?"

But Jesus looked at them and said, "With men it is impossible, but not with God; for with God all things are possible."

As you can see in this passage of scripture, when the young man asks for eternal life, Jesus' first response was, "Keep the commandments." And the young man said, "Master, all these have I kept from my youth."

Now, I believe that the young man's habit of keeping the commandments is the reason he had become prosperous. Remember what God said in Deuteronomy 8:18 — *And you shall remember the Lord your God, for it is He who gives you power to get wealth, that He may establish His covenant which He swore to your fathers, as it is this day.*

Who is it that empowers us to prosper? It's God! He moves in our lives and in our circumstances as we invite Him in to do so. And we invite Him in through obedience to and faith in His Word. Let me point out that there is no substitute for keeping God's commandments. Jesus said He came to fulfill the law, not to replace it (Matthew 5:17). The word *fulfill* means "fully filled, having no lack."

Jesus came to complete us, to remove the lack from our lives, but He didn't do away with the commandments, because they are still true. They are a part of God's ways of doing and being, so they are necessary for us to walk in God's provision and prosperity.

So, as this young ruler obeyed God's Word, he became prosperous. But even though he was rich, he still sensed that he lacked something. That's why he came to Jesus, seeking His help.

Mark 10:21 says, *Then Jesus, looking at him, loved him.* Jesus didn't stop loving him because he had money. Do you see it? Jesus is not against people having money. As Deuteronomy says, it is God who gives people the ability to earn money. And His purpose in giving us this ability is so that we can establish His covenant — His kingdom — in the earth.

Catch What Jesus Is Really Saying Here

Out of His love for the young man, Jesus said to him, *One thing you lack: Go your way, sell whatever you have and give to the poor, and you will have treasure in heaven; and come, take up the cross, and follow Me* (v. 21).

In other words, He was saying, "You're wondering what you've been lacking. You wonder why you feel you still need something, in spite of your obedience to God's Word and your prosperity. Here's why you feel that way, and here's what you can do about it. You can *give*, and trust Me."

I believe this is where the rubber meets the road, not just for the young ruler, but for you and me today as well. How will we respond when Jesus asks us to give? Mark 10:22 tells us the rich young ruler was saddened: *But he was sad at this word, and went away sorrowful, for he had great possessions.*

Now, here is where many people get hung up and miss the point. They misunderstand it. But I want you to catch this — Jesus wasn't saying that people who have wealth can't get to

Heaven. If that were true, then everybody would have to be poor in order to serve the Lord.

But this is not what the Bible teaches us. The scripture actually says that God *delights* in the prosperity of His children (Psalm 35:27). He takes pleasure in seeing us thriving and living an abundant life. That's what Jesus came to give us, and it pleases Him when He sees us enjoying His gift.

Consider Abraham, Isaac, and Jacob — three righteous men who served God and are examples to us of righteous living today. All three men had wealth. Genesis 13:2 tells us that Abraham *was very rich in livestock, in silver, and in gold*. His son, Isaac, was also wealthy; Genesis 26:13–14 says Isaac *began to prosper, and continued prospering until he became very prosperous; for he had possessions of flocks and possessions of herds and a great number of servants.* Abraham's grandson, Jacob, was even more successful. He helped his father-in-law Laban to prosper as well as becoming greatly wealthy himself (Genesis 30:30, 43).

So, what was the difference between the rich young ruler and these three mighty patriarchs of Israel? I believe the difference is where they placed their trust, their faith. Abraham, Isaac, and Jacob had riches, but they didn't place their trust in their riches. They put their faith not in money, but in God, who gave them that money.

The rich young ruler had gained his wealth the same way Abraham, Isaac, and Jacob had — obeying God. But somewhere along the line, he had changed his source. In times past, he had kept God's commands, and God had prospered him. Now, though, he had turned from God and was trusting in his wealth to be his source.

I believe that's what Jesus was really telling the young man: "You're trusting in the wrong source. So, give that wealth away and follow Me again." The young man couldn't do it. He couldn't give and trust God to receive back again. So, he walked away.

At this point, Jesus said to His disciples, *How difficult it will be for those who are wealthy [and cling to possessions and status as security] to enter the kingdom of God* (Mark 10:23 AMP). Really, what Jesus was saying is this: "How impossible it is for people who *trust* in their money as their source to be saved."

That's the reason this man went away with deep sadness in his heart. He was trusting in his money instead of the Lord. Then he felt this as a lack, a need, in his life, but when Jesus addressed the issue, the young man found it too difficult to go back to trusting in God.

The issue isn't that God doesn't want to supply all our needs according to His riches in glory. The issue is that when we place our trust in material things like money, we are not fully trusting in God. We can only put our trust in one thing. And that one thing will be the god we serve. We can serve God, or we can serve money. But we can't serve both.

In the very first commandment, God said, *"You shall have no other gods before me"* (Exodus 20:3). That means we are to make sure that God is always first in our lives. But all too often, people begin to place their trust in money and riches. They see the riches as meeting their needs, and they can be tempted to forget God.

I believe that's what happened to the rich young ruler. He started looking to his riches as his source, and God was no longer first in his life. His money became a god to him, and so he had broken God's commandment not to have any other god *before Him*. Jesus saw it and said, "This is why it's impossible for people to get to Heaven if they are trusting in riches or anything else as a source. God is the only source. He is the only God. He is the only One who can save us."

It's Not Either/Or

Here is the good news. We don't have to make a choice between God or having the money we need to pay our bills and enjoy life. It's not either God or money. It's all about who and what we trust and have faith in.

Notice that the disciples were astonished at the whole situation, and they asked Jesus, "Who then can be saved?" Many people equate riches and success with God's favor. If a person is wealthy, they think, then the person must be right with God. And certainly, it can seem to many people that it would be easier to serve God if you had a lot of money in the bank. How easy it is to give tithes and offerings if you have a large bank account.

But remember — God isn't pleased with money. He is pleased with our faith (Hebrews 11:6). So, Jesus answered the disciples and said, *"With men it is impossible, but not with God: for with God all things are possible"* (Mark 10:26–27). We can't be saved through our wealth. But with God, all things are possible. We can be both saved and prosperous, if we are trusting God as our source.

At this point, Peter spoke up and said, *"See, we have left all and followed You"* (Mark 10:28). I believe he was saying, "Jesus, we have put everything aside and put God first in our lives. He's our source. We have stopped trusting in anything except You. Will we get anything out of it? What's in it for us?"

Remember, Peter and the disciples were still grappling with how a person might be saved, and how God would show His favor to them. Peter wanted to know, "If having riches isn't an automatic sign of God's favor, then what is?"

Now, God does not ask us to put Him first and then expect nothing in return. Jesus was quick to answer Peter with an encouraging word: *"Assuredly, I say to you, there is no one who has left house or brothers or sisters or father or mother or wife or children or lands, for My sake and the gospel's, who shall not receive a hundredfold NOW IN THIS TIME—houses and brothers and sisters and mothers and children and lands, with persecutions—and in the age to come, eternal life"* (Mark 10:29–30).

I believe Jesus was explaining to Peter, and to us, that we are to put things in proper order in our lives. As we put God and His Word first, trusting Him as the source of our total supply, then He will add all the things we need to our lives (Matthew 6:33). His eternal law of prosperity will work exactly as it has from the beginning of creation. Nobody who turns from trusting material things or other people as their source will lose out. God tells us we will receive something from Him in return. Our needs will be met, through Him.

Catch this: Jesus never expected His disciples, then or now, to live in poverty. Deuteronomy does not say, "It is God who gives you power to get poverty." It says He gives us the power to get wealth — and that means prosperity, abundance, our needs met, and our lack filled. God doesn't want you to suffer with sickness, loneliness, worry, guilt, fear, depression, or lack. He wants you to have His best in all things.

We do not need to be poor or defeated to be a Christian. Poverty and suffering do not please God. I believe it is good for us to have friends, loved ones, real estate, money, health, influence, and other blessings. We can have them, but they shouldn't have us. They shouldn't have such a hold over our heart that we fail to serve God and obey Him.

Once we make Jesus our personal Savior, give Him our best seed and look only to Him as our Lord and Savior, then I believe we have a Bible right to expect a harvest from Him. Jesus personally and clearly promised us in Mark 10:30 His hundredfold return — a harvest of everything we need in life — as we follow Him with our whole heart. And because He has promised to care for us, I believe we have a biblical right to attack our lack, in faith, expecting miracles.

In This Life

I've heard some Christians say, "I'll be rich when I get to Heaven." But in Heaven, we won't have a need for riches, because there won't be any poverty.

In Heaven, we won't lack anything that costs money. Heaven itself is rich and abundant, and everything we need will automatically be ours. Jesus has already paid for it all. We will have health, love, time, beauty, energy, and joy. And so will everyone else. The struggles we face on earth will be over. We won't need riches once we get to Heaven.

And we don't have to lack any good thing down here to qualify for good things in Heaven. Lack isn't how we are saved, any more than prosperity is.

That's why Jesus tells us in Mark 10:29–30 that He has a harvest for us *in this life*. He doesn't demand that we be poor on earth so we can make it to Heaven. I encourage you to study Mark 10 and let it get into your heart and stir your faith so you can begin to declare by faith, "I'm blessed. All my needs are being met according to His riches in glory."

And as your needs are met, enjoy your life. Enjoy your blessings. Continually thank God for what you have and worship Him and seek Him. Remember, God intends for you to be blessed in every area of your life. You don't have to accept your lack. You can come against lack with faith, courage, and determination so that you can accomplish all He has called you to do.

Have You Made God Your Source?

Now, you may be saying, "Richard, I don't know if God is my source. I don't know that I've ever made Him my source. I've been trusting in other things, other people, instead of in God. What do I need to do?"

If that's you, then I encourage you right now to turn your life fully over to God. When you give your life to Him, then He will become your source. And you can know for sure where you stand with Him.

I encourage you to decide firmly right now that you are going to put God first. Accept God's plan for your life by accepting Jesus into your heart as your Lord and Savior. Ask Him to save you and fill you with His Holy Spirit. Ask Him to help you every day of your life to keep Him as your source.

How do you do this? It's simple — just talk to Him. Speak to Him just as you would speak to a person who is there in the room with you. You can say this prayer or one like it:

"God, I know I haven't been putting You first in my life, but I want to. I'm sorry I've put other things before You. Please forgive me, and cleanse me from all sin. I want to make a new beginning right now. I believe that Jesus is Your Son. I ask Him into my heart right now. I receive Him as Savior and Lord. Fill me with Your Holy Spirit. Teach me to do things the way You do them, to think the way You think, to give to You in faith and expect harvests from You by faith. In Jesus' Name, I pray. Amen."

Now that you have prayed this prayer, I encourage you to continue studying the Word of God, praying, worshipping God, and keeping Him first in your life. Make the confession every day that you are trusting in Him as your source to meet your needs.

Remember These Principles

- God is the One who empowers us to prosper.

- As we obey God's Word, we can begin to prosper and thrive in our lives.

- As we prosper, we must remember to keep God first in our lives.

- We can serve God and enjoy prosperity at the same time, as long as we continue to trust God instead of trusting in our riches.

- If you haven't been putting God first in your life, you can pray and begin doing so right now.

CHAPTER TWELVE

Do You Want Miracles by the Teaspoon or the Truckload?

My wife, Lindsay, likes to cook. My daughter, Jordan, does as well. Over the years, as I have watched Lindsay and Jordan cook and bake, I have seen how familiar and comfortable they are with measurements — which is a vital part of cooking and baking foods that taste as they should.

When they're cooking, Lindsay and Jordan use measuring cups and spoons and other kitchen tools to mix all the ingredients just right. They may add in a cup of this, or a spoonful of that, or a pinch of something else into the recipe. I watch in amazement as they work, admiring how they make their favorite dishes come together.

And of course, I especially enjoy it when the meal is cooked, and it is placed on the table so I can eat it. I get to enjoy the delicious taste of what they have made. I don't have to know the exact measurements they have used to make the recipe come together so well — but after years of watching them in the kitchen, I've learned one thing for sure:

Measuring the right amounts of every ingredient into the mix is essential to having a meal that tastes amazing.

God Knows the Right Measurement
to Meet Your Need

I used the example above because it is easy to get a visual image of how important it is to measure things precisely. And God, in His goodness and His attention to all the details of our lives, knows how to give us what we need in just the right, divine measure to meet our needs and give us an overflow. How do I know this? I know it because I know what He said in Luke 6:38.

Luke 6:38 (NIV)

Give, and it will be given to you. A good amount will be poured into your lap. It will be pressed down, shaken together, and running over. The same amount you give will be measured out to you.

In this verse, God is revealing something very important and powerful when it comes to how we give and receive in His kingdom. As the giver, *we* are the one who determines the measure, or extent, of how people will give to us. *The same amount you give will be measured out to you.*

So, let me ask you this:

Do you want God's miracles poured back to you by the spoonful, the cupful, the barrel-full, or the truckload-full?

I believe Jesus is telling us that the way we give — the measure that we give by — is what determines the measure that we receive when God meets our needs. He may use our jobs, our friends, our family, or perfect strangers to get a harvest into our hands. But it's not our boss, our friends, our family, or other people who choose what we reap from our seeds. It is you and I who are determining what measure we reap by. And we determine that measure by the measure we use to give.

You could say it this way: Are you giving by the spoonful? Are you sowing seeds by the cupful? Or are you giving by the barrel-full or the truckload-full? Whatever you're sowing, however much you're sowing, that's how much you'll reap. Give a little, get a little. Give a lot, harvest a lot. Sow nothing… reap nothing.

And when God is talking about the measure we use to give, I believe He's not talking about the exact dollar amount. He's talking about *how* we give. Are we giving to God with a cheerful heart, as 2 Corinthians 9:7 tells us to do? Are we giving because we feel we have to — out of obligation instead of a desire to give? Are we giving to show off and gain the approval of others? What is our reason for giving?

I believe our motivation behind our giving is what matters to God. And I also believe that God is looking for faith in us. How much faith does it take for us to give? Are we giving an amount that is easy for us to give? Or are we giving even when it's not so easy in the natural to give, because we love God and trust Him to meet our needs?

That's what I believe we see at work in the life of the poor widow whose story we read in Mark 12:41–44. Jesus was in the temple one day when He saw this widow arrive to give her offering to the Lord. All around her, people with much more riches than she had were giving their tithes. Then the woman approached the altar and gave two mites — two tiny copper coins that weren't worth very much. It would have been like tossing two pennies into the offering.

Yet Jesus turned to His disciples and said, *"Assuredly, I say to you that this poor widow has put in more than all those who have given to the treasury; for they all put in out of their abundance, but she out of her poverty put in all that she had, her whole livelihood"* (v. 43–44).

In other words, I believe He was saying, "Notice what just happened. This poor widow has given more than everyone else here today."

Mathematically, of course, she hadn't given more. Comparing

just the dollar amounts would show you that others had given a bigger check, so to speak. But God doesn't look at the amount — He looks at the heart. And in her heart, this woman had given her all. She had given out of her need, trusting God with everything she had.

In fact, it says she gave her whole livelihood. It was all she had. And it takes faith to give that way. It takes faith to give that generously. And what does the Bible say about faith? It says God sees what we do in faith, and He rewards it.

Don't Shut God Out of Your Giving

My dad used to tell a story about trusting God during our giving. I'm going to share it here:

"A brother in the Lord began to prosper in a big way. At the same time, he was given the opportunity to plant big. His wife was ready. But he went to his accountant, who told him he shouldn't give big because of tax reasons.

"When the man asked me my opinion of tithing, I asked him, 'Are you a tither and were you ever a tither?'

"The man said, 'I was before I got this kind of money.'

"I asked, 'You aren't now?' He said no. So I said, 'I advise you to pray about this and remember who your source is. A rejected opportunity to give is a lost opportunity to receive.'

"That statement came to me with such force that it surprised me. I felt like this brother was in trouble. He was a tither, and previously God has blessed him in a big way. But now he had stopped giving, and he didn't seem to care.

"I know one thing for certain: by shutting God out of our giving, we also shut Him out of our receiving."

To me, this story is powerful because it reminds us that we must continually stay in faith concerning every area of our lives, including our giving and receiving. When we start to look to means other than God to meet our needs, we are not exercising our faith in Him as our source. And when we're not using our faith, it's not very likely that we'll receive the harvests we need from Him. He must have our faith to work with.

How Much Are You Willing to Risk to Receive a Harvest?

Many times, people can get hung up and worried over the circumstances so much that they become afraid to give. Maybe they are looking at their bank account and feel like they can't afford to give. Maybe giving feels too risky.

But the measure we use to give is the measure by which we will receive. So, if we are being led by God to take a step of faith and give big, it's important to do it.

God Himself is the perfect example of this. Consider the measure He used when He gave His Son, Jesus, on the Cross for us. He had only one begotten Son. To give that Son was huge, it was generous, and it could have even seemed risky. After all, how many of us would have done the same?

He could have decided to give something else instead of Jesus. For example, He could have given one or more of the uncounted number of angels He created. It might have seemed easier, or less risky, to do so.

But that kind of giving wasn't enough for the harvest God was expecting to receive. He wanted the best harvest He could get — the redemption of mankind, the forgiveness of our sin for all time. What He wanted was big, so He gave big. God gave His very best, His only Son, Jesus.

God didn't try to figure out how little He could give. He focused on how much He could give. God didn't give something He would hardly miss. Instead, He gave up the One who would cost Him the most to give up!

God risked everything for you and me to be saved.

That's the God-kind of giving. And because of it, He has you, me, and millions of others redeemed back to Him. He gave His Son's life to get your life and my life. God gave His most precious Son, Jesus, in order to receive back the most precious possession — you and me!

Giving Doesn't Mean Losing; It Means Gaining

Now, I want you to notice something. God doesn't lose what He gives. Jesus lived a sinless life, gave Himself for us on the Cross, paid the price for our sins, died, was raised again, ascended to Heaven, and is now seated at the right hand of God. God still has His only begotten Son — because He gave Him.

I believe we also will have, because we give. We won't lose out when we give. With God, we'll gain a harvest that is thirty-, sixty-, a hundredfold back (Mark 4:20). Talk about increase!

In the God-kind of giving and receiving, this is the way the measurement system works. It works by the law of multiplication. God multiplies back to us what we give to Him in good measure, pressed down to fullness, shaken together, and running over so we have an overflow.

God is still receiving people into His kingdom today because He gave the gift of Jesus. God gave for a desired result, and He is still getting that desired result every hour, every day. He's receiving lost souls back unto Himself, and seeing us healed, delivered, and restored from the clutches of Satan.

God receives according to the measure He used when He gave. And He receives back a harvest from what He gave. He hasn't lost anything; He's only gained from His giving.

I hope this encourages you to look closely at what you have and what you need right now, and to give your best seed every time you sow toward your harvests. When God receives our best seed, He gives His best harvest back to us. As we receive that harvest from Him, we are able to come against our lack and defeat it.

Remember These Principles

- A rejected opportunity to give is a lost opportunity to receive.

- We receive according to the measure we give by.

- The God-kind of giving is to give generously, in faith, to receive the harvest we need.

- If we want the best results from our giving, then we need to give our best.

CHAPTER THIRTEEN

The God-Kind of Prosperity and the Man-Kind of Prosperity — There Is a Difference

The degree to which God prospers us depends on us giving and receiving as God does — in faith, generously, giving our best. We are not to give and receive like mankind gives and receives. The God-kind of giving and receiving has a blessing attached to it that goes far beyond the visible treasures of this earth.

Many Christians don't know what that blessing is, because they don't realize that there are two types of prosperity — the God-kind and the man-kind. One kind will set you free, while the other can bind you up and cause you to miss out on what God has for you.

I'm here to tell you that the God-kind of increase is far better than anything that comes to us the world's way. The man-kind of prosperity pales in comparison to the God-kind.

What Is the Man-Kind of Prosperity?

There is a distinct difference between getting our needs met in people-centered ways and receiving the supply for all our needs through God's way.

When we strive to get something without depending on God to be involved to make it happen, we end up dissatisfied. I believe this is because what truly satisfies us deep down inside is something *spiritual*. We have a need for God and His ways of doing and being that nothing else can fill.

So, when we receive earthly things yet we don't have faith at work in us, we aren't fully satisfied. We can never be fully satisfied if we're seeking after things rather than seeking after God. We might have something that meets a need — like money or a car or a house — but it won't fully fill and satisfy every part of us the way God's presence can.

I remember my dad telling the story of a wonderful, successful man who had devoted his life to working diligently to obtain earthly things. The man was gracious and friendly, but when it came to giving, he could not find it within himself to give time or money to the Lord's work.

As this man was showing Dad his beautiful vacation house, he waved his hand at the house, and said, "Oral, this is what it's all about. This is why I work so hard to earn money. I want to enjoy it." He almost seemed to be under a spell. That was the kind of grip these material possessions had on him.

In comparison, I thought of the years I watched Dad give to God not only financially, but in all aspects of his life. Dad had to learn how to walk in the God-kind of prosperity. He had to learn what the Word of God said, then apply it to his life in faith, and expect miracles. He learned to expect miracles every day, which is how he came to teach others how to do so too.

The Man-Kind of Prosperity Doesn't Last

For a time, the successful, wealthy man my father had met was doing well for himself. Then one day, Dad received an urgent call from the man, who desperately wanted to see him. He told Dad he was on the verge of losing everything, and he asked for his help to get him back on track financially.

Dad was astounded at this turn of events. The man had earned millions of dollars over the years and had kept all he earned. As far as Dad knew, the man wasn't wasting money, yet he still found himself in a financial crisis, and he was suddenly desperate.

My dad said he was flattered on the one hand to have the man seeking him for financial advice, but saddened on the other hand. This man understood receiving but could not understand what it meant to be a giver. And somehow, in the midst of all of his receiving, he was losing everything financially.

The Place of Miracles

Dad was reminded of something the man had said years earlier concerning his ministry. He said, "Oral, I don't believe in miracles."

Dad replied, "You will when you need one."

Now, as Dad was talking to him in the middle of the crisis, the man started to say it once again. "Oral, I don't believe in miracles." But he caught himself. He said instead, "I believe in miracles, but they sure cost, don't they?"

Dad said, "Yes, miracles cost God the giving of His only begotten Son, Jesus. Our giving costs us too. Without giving, both on God's part and our part, there are no miracles. Without planting our seed, there will be no miracle harvest, the kind that counts when the chips are down."

That day for the first time, my dad's friend became a giver. And you can imagine the rest of the story. That day, he began to expect a miracle and to receive the miracles he so desperately needed.

The God-Kind of Giving Makes Us More Like God

Giving is God's nature, His character, and the essence of His being. It's not in His nature to keep everything for Himself. What He has, He freely gives. Jesus said God even clothes the lilies of the field and is concerned when a lowly sparrow falls. (See Matthew 6:25–34; Matthew 10:29–31.)

I've heard people say, "It's hard for me to believe in God. It's hard for me to trust Him."

I tell them what I heard Dad say about it: "My problem is not believing in God, but that He believes in me."

It's amazing, even overwhelming, to realize that God believes so much in us. But when we understand how much God cares about us, believes in us, and wants to see us prosper and succeed, we can find it easier to walk with Him, to talk with Him, to act on His Word in faith, and be like Him in our everyday lives.

The God-Kind of Giving Is Based on Love

God can work in and through us when we sow to Him. And as He works in and through us, He is able to expand His kingdom on earth. After we accept Jesus into our hearts as Lord and Savior, we are filled with God's Holy Spirit — and that means that we have extended God's Spirit on this earth through one more life. We have expanded God's influence in the world. We are one more witness of His power and love.

God's very nature, the essence of Who He is, is that He *loves* so much that He gives (John 3:16). As we consider the God-kind of loving, giving, and receiving, we can see that His way of doing and being can be our ways of doing and being too. His nature can also become our nature.

We can begin loving, giving, and receiving like God does. We can "so love that we give."

The God-Kind of Giving Results in Joy

Now, I believe the God-kind of giving is not meant to be a one-way street. God gives. He always gives. And while He'll never force us to do something, He does expect that as He gives into our lives, it will spur us to give back. He has faith that His giving will produce results.

Yes, God gives. But He also receives. He receives as a result of His giving. It is His giving into humanity that generates what He receives from those who receive His gift. The seeds God sows come back to Him in harvests of those who accept Jesus and are saved.

When someone accepts Jesus as their Savior, God gets a part of humanity back into His kingdom. This is what I mean when I say that God's giving is a two-way street. He gives and receives. He sows and reaps.

Jesus reminds us that when a sinner recognizes God's gift of salvation and is saved, *"There is joy in the presence of the angels of God over one sinner who repents"* (Luke 15:10). If there is joy among God's angels over one of us repenting and returning to God, think of the joy that God gets when we return to Him. There is joy in giving, because there is joy in receiving.

The God-Kind of Giving and Receiving Involves People

Whenever we give into God's kingdom to further His work in the earth, we are giving to God Himself. And God alone chooses how He will send our harvest back to us. He works through people to bless our giving back to us. They may be the people we expect to give back to us, or they may not be. But when God chooses, it's just right.

This is one reason why it's so important to look to God for our harvest, not to man. The means God uses to bless us and send us a harvest may change. He may do it in a way we would never begin to imagine. But He will surely do it.

As we pursue the God-kind of prosperity, we are coming against our lack His way, not man's. When we are obedient to sow our seeds according to God's Word and His will, we will receive a harvest. God has our harvest under control. He is doing the multiplying of our seed sown in faith. And we will reap a harvest in due season. This means as we obey Him, we have a Bible right to thrive in His abundance.

Remember These Principles

- The God-kind of giving and receiving has a blessing attached to it that goes far beyond the visible treasures of this earth.
- Giving is God's nature, His character, and the essence of His being.
- God will work in and through us when we sow to Him.
- It's important to look to God for our harvest, not to man.

CHAPTER FOURTEEN

Have You Heard About the Man Who Sowed in Difficult Times and Reaped a Hundredfold Harvest?

God's Word tells us to sow our seeds continually. We are to give in both good times and bad times. In good times, we may have more to give than in bad times, but in either case we are to give as a seed we sow, expecting to receive a harvest. As we continue to get seed after seed into the ground, we can begin to expect harvest after harvest to come. We can get into a rhythm of continually giving and receiving.

There are two reasons for us to give in good times. First of all, we give because we are thankful for the abundance we have. Second, we give so that we put more seeds into the ground, so that God's supply will continue to come in. Our continual giving creates a heavenly storehouse for God's supply to be there when we need to call forth a harvest.

Philippians 4:13–19 says that when we sow our seeds unto God, we are putting a deposit into our heavenly account. Then as we have need, we can remind ourselves how we have faithfully been giving to God. We can look to the Lord of the harvest, and believe that He is multiplying our seed back to us to meet our need.

Cashing in Our Receipt with God

My dad used to call the seeds we sow a receipt in our heavenly account. Malachi 3 says that when we bring our tithe into God's storehouse, He opens the windows of Heaven and pours out to us a blessing so great, there is not room enough to receive it all. This speaks of our giving and receiving.

As Dad studied Malachi 3, he found that one translation said it as "giving and receipting." Those words were a lovely thought until one day he found himself in the emergency room needing a miracle.

It started when he came into the house one night and told my mother that he was having terrible cramps. They prayed, but the cramping grew worse. When they called the doctor, the doctor listened to Dad's symptoms and then said, "Oral, you have appendicitis." And he ordered him to go immediately to the emergency room.

As they drove to the hospital, they both prayed and waited to hear from God. Then a thought came to Dad. He remembered how Philippians 4 describes our giving as making deposits into a heavenly account.

He turned to my mother and said, "We've planted a lot of seeds of faith into the Gospel and into the lives of other people. And you know we have receipts in Heaven that we can cash in. Agree in prayer with me that I am cashing in a receipt with the Lord tonight for my healing. I'm believing that I won't have to have surgery." They agreed in prayer for a miracle healing.

When Dad got to the emergency room, he was still in severe pain. The ER doctor examined him and confirmed that it was appendicitis. "The surgeon is on his way," he said. Then Dad had tests that also confirmed the diagnosis of appendicitis. His appendix was enlarged and inflamed, and it needed to come out.

At every turn, Dad kept confessing God's Word and reminding the Lord that he was cashing in his receipt for healing. Every time he heard the diagnosis repeated, Dad had a choice — to get discouraged and give up, or to persist in expecting what he had prayed for, even when the circumstances looked negative.

Just when it seemed there wasn't anything else to be done but to have the surgery, a miracle happened. The ultrasound technician and the doctor watched as the ultrasound screen began to change. It was as though a cloud had come over the screen, and when it cleared, Dad's appendix no longer looked enlarged or enflamed. The pain left too.

The doctor could hardly believe what he'd seen with his own eyes, but he couldn't deny it. He confirmed that Dad didn't have appendicitis anymore. He had been healed. And he didn't have to have surgery, just as he had prayed and agreed with my mother.

Expecting to Receive from God Is Biblical

The Bible teaches this in Genesis. Abraham gave to God. In fact, the Bible says he gave "tithes of all" (Genesis 14:20). And from the seeds Abraham sowed, God brought about a mighty harvest. He gave Abraham and his wife Sarah a son, Isaac, when it seemed impossible in the natural for them to have a child.

Then God told Abraham to teach his son, Isaac, about giving in both good times and bad times. Isaac learned the lesson so well, he literally sowed in famine.

We see this account of Isaac's amazing giving and receiving in Genesis 26:1–4. At the time, there was a severe famine in the land. Isaac remember that his father, Abraham, had experienced famine. But he had continued to give of what he had to God, no matter how little it was.

By his faith, Abraham refused to waver in his giving because of his circumstances. He gave God tithes of all he had. He gave first out of gratitude for what God had given him; second, he gave as a seed to yield a continual harvest from God. And Isaac saw his father do this, and it built faith in him.

When we trust God as our source as Abraham did, then whether we face good times or bad times, we are not going to be affected by our circumstances in the same way that the world is. We won't be subject to the same ups and downs as those who look to the economy or to themselves as their source.

Our giving is to be continual, daily, monthly, yearly. We must be steady and consistent in sowing our seed and believing for our harvest. Giving and believing go together. As James 2:20 tells us, *faith without works is dead*. Seed and faith are two sides of the same coin.

What About the Faith Side?

If we want our faith to be stable and productive, then we must root and ground our faith in God's Word. Then and only then will our faith have the staying power we need to stand against the devil until he flees and our circumstances turn around for our good.

How do we get that kind of faith? Romans 10:17 gives us the answer: *Faith comes by hearing, and hearing by the Word of God.* In Matthew 17:20, Jesus explained it by saying: *"If you have faith as a mustard seed, you will say to this mountain, 'Move from here to there,' and it will move; and nothing will be impossible for you."*

Our faith is like a seed, just as our giving is like a seed. A seed is ultimately what every living thing comes from. Seeds are the carriers of life. For our faith to come alive, it must work like a seed. It must be planted in the soil of God's Word. It must grow. It must produce fruit. And it's hearing the Word of God that causes the seed of our faith to begin to grow.

We are to confess God's Word in faith as we sow the seeds of our giving. We are to sow our seeds of faith in the good soil of God's work. And then we can speak to our mountain of need and command it to be removed and believe it will obey us!

Isaac Had Steady Faith and Steady Giving

When Isaac saw the famine in the land, he initially wanted to leave and go to Egypt where there was said to be plenty of food to meet his needs. But instead, God talked to him about seed sowing. God instructed Isaac to stay where he was and plant his seeds right there.

At first, it must have been mind-boggling for Isaac to grasp. Imagine it. God was telling him to plant seed in dry earth. There was no rain and no promise of rain anytime soon. Famine had hit the land. Everyone was experiencing bad times, Isaac among them. By all natural indications, it was the wrong time and wrong place to plant seed, expecting it to grow.

Isaac was faced with a decision. Would he obey God? Or would he get up and run to Egypt?

Genesis 26:2–3

Then the Lord appeared to him and said: "Do not go down to Egypt; live in the land of which I shall tell you. Dwell in this land, and I will be with you and bless you; for to you and your descendants I give all these lands, and I will perform the oath which I swore to Abraham your father."

In other words, God said, "Isaac, stay in the land I have given your father Abraham. Don't move. Hold steady. I will bless you there. I will multiply your seed. I will do it because I have a covenant with Abraham. Remember how I took care of Abraham. Remember how he kept My commandments. I will take care of you the same way if you sow your seed."

So, Isaac decided to sow.

Genesis 26:12

Then Isaac sowed in that land, and reaped in the same year a hundredfold; and the Lord blessed him.

Isaac made the decision to believe God. Once he believed, then he acted. He sowed actual seed, in faith. He didn't hold back, but sowed even when everyone around him would not.

In the natural realm, it must have looked as though Isaac was setting himself up for failure. After all, seeds don't grow in soil that has had no water and is hard and unproductive. But in the spirit realm where God works and creates, Isaac's faith was working as a seed in the good soil of God's promise to him.

And Isaac not only sowed his seed but he also reaped a harvest in the same year — a hundredfold harvest, the best harvest possible from the seeds he sowed. Hallelujah!

Risk Everything to Do What God Says

To sow in famine and reap a hundredfold harvest, Isaac had to take a huge step of faith. He gave out of his need and risked everything to obey God. He had to trust God to be the source that would produce the harvest, because the earth was in no condition to make those seeds grow in the natural realm. He trusted God to give him a harvest even if it took a miracle.

And that's exactly what he received — a miraculous, hundredfold harvest in the same year he sowed.

Notice, Isaac sowed according to God's Word to him. He was not acting out of presumption or foolishness. He didn't say, "Well, I'm going to sow just to show people it can be done." Isaac sowed in faith that He had heard God's Word to him.

What Does God Say to Us Today?

One of the most interesting things I see happening in Genesis 26 is that God didn't let Isaac back off from his seed sowing, even when the circumstances looked terrible. God encouraged Isaac to trust Him even in hard times, just as his father Abraham did.

By listening to God instead of focusing on how the circumstances appeared, Isaac was able to receive a harvest according to God's promise. Matthew 6:33 says that when we sow first by seeking the kingdom of God and His ways of doing and being, all the things we have need of shall be added to us. God was asking Isaac to put Him first in order to receive His blessing.

It would have been easy for Isaac to ignore God's Word to him and do things his own way. And sometimes, it can feel easier for us to do things our way too, leaving God out of the picture. But if we leave Him out of the picture, we leave Him out of our solution too.

I believe God is telling us that we can follow Isaac's example today. What did Isaac do? He listened to God, sowed as God told him to, and stood firm until he received his harvest. And he received God's best.

Likewise, you and I can sow as God tells us to, even if times are tough. Remember, *God is the same yesterday, today, and forever* (Hebrews 13:8). So, the question is: What is God saying to us, and will we answer with obedience or excuses? Isaac heard God's Word and allowed his excuses to become obedience.

His father Abraham was faced with a similar decision of obedience or disobedience when God promised him a son. That son was Isaac. Romans 4:20 tells us that Abraham did not stagger or waver at the promises of God in unbelief. Instead, he believed and expected a miracle. And God's promise of a son came to pass because Abraham chose to obey.

And just like Abraham, God gives us the power, the ability, to choose to obey or disobey Him. We can choose to hear His Word or disregard it. Abraham attached his faith to his choices, and God requires the same of us. We can believe that circumstances will never change, or we can trust God and believe His Word, regardless of the circumstances.

We have a choice to make. As Joshua 24:15 says, *Choose this day whom you will serve.* And I love the end of that scripture because it says, *As for me and my house, we will serve the Lord.* That's the choice that brings about miraculous harvests.

God Doesn't Want Us to Be in Poverty

God doesn't want us to be poor and lacking anything we need spiritually, physically, or financially. God desires to meet all our needs according to His riches in glory by Christ Jesus. He wants us to get into the continual rhythm of seedtime and harvest — the God-kind of giving and receiving. God wants to bless us. He wants to bless *you.* He wants you to thrive in His blessings.

God told Isaac, "I will cause your seed to multiply." God's laws of seedtime and harvest, giving and receiving, and the multiplication of our seeds for a harvest don't change. They are always the same. If we sow to God in faith, according to His Word and His will, the seed will multiply, whether we sow in famine or in great conditions.

God also told Isaac, "I will do what I say because of My covenant." What is the covenant God has with us today? It's the shed blood of Jesus Christ. God is saying to us, "I will take care of you and multiply your seed sown in faith to meet your needs because of your relationship with Jesus."

How Do You Give in Famine?

So, how do we give when we are facing lack so overwhelming that it seems we don't even have any seed to sow? The Bible says that God gives seed to the sower (2 Corinthians 9:10). When we put our faith in God and we want to sow, we can ask God to give us seed to sow. He will give us some of what we lack so we can use it against our need.

Whatever you lack right now — finances, friends, a job, a home, a car, good health, whatever it may be — ask God to give you seed to sow toward it. If you lack money, ask God for finances to sow into His kingdom. Do you lack friends? Look at the people around you. God may direct you to give one of them a friendly word or a smile. Do you lack time? You have 24 hours a day. Consider setting aside some time, even if it is just a few minutes, to give in some way that furthers God's work on this earth.

You may be thinking, "I can't afford to give." I understand that kind of thinking. We all face times when our needs look so great, it's hard to imagine being able to give. But we can't afford not to give! Sowing our seed is how we receive a harvest from God. If we're not sowing, how can we reap?

When I have a need, I know it's time to give something toward that need. I know I must put some seed into God's hands so that He can multiply it back to me, good measure, pressed down, shaken together and running over. That's the only way we can effectively use our faith to come against our lack and receive a harvest from God and begin to thrive in His abundance. This principle will work — if we will work it, by faith!

Remember These Principles

- We are to sow the seeds of our time, our love, our faith, and our finances in all seasons, in good times and bad times.
- As we give to God in faith, it's as if we're making deposits into a heavenly bank account. When we pray for a need to be met, it is like making a withdrawal or cashing in a receipt with God.
- No matter how big a need may be, if we seek God for an answer and then do what He says to do, we can expect harvests — thirty-, sixty-, and even hundredfold harvests.
- The choice to do what God tells us to do is always up to us. As we act on His Word in faith, we can expect the harvests we need and thrive in Him.

CONCLUSION

CHAPTER FIFTEEN

Roses Will Bloom Again!

My dad used to share a message about God's goodness that I'd like to share with you now.

One day, a pastor went to pray for a man who was suffering with a bad case of arthritis. Now, arthritis can be terribly crippling and painful. This sick man's joints were badly swollen, and he was in constant pain. A doctor would come each week to give him treatments and see to his physical needs. The pastor would come to pray and see to the man's spiritual needs.

But in spite of the medicine, the prayers, and the ministrations of the doctor, the man wasn't experiencing an improvement in his condition. He began to believe he would never get better. His spirit became downcast. He was defeated. He stopped smiling, and he became terribly bitter.

The neighbors who had been bringing food stopped showing up, because the man didn't welcome them anymore. He pushed everyone away from him in his pain and discouragement and bitterness. The only person who still spent time with him was his nurse. And even she didn't want to be there because he was so bitter and hard to deal with.

When the pastor visited the man in his downcast state, he tried to cheer him up. He spoke encouragingly. But the man lay on his bed, curled up in himself. He refused to look at the pastor. He refused to speak. He wouldn't smile. The pastor wanted desperately to reach the sick man at least one more time in the hope that his prayers would bring about a breakthrough. While the pastor was still by the man's bedside, the doctor arrived.

The doctor examined the sick man, treated him with more medicine, and then he said:

"Right now, you're a very sick man. But I've been thinking of all the good things you've done with your life. And I've got good news for you."

The sick man whispered, "You do?"

The doctor nodded. "I have a new medicine that's going to turn your life around, and you're going to be amazed by its results."

"Do you have it with you? For God's sake, doctor, give it to me."

The doctor smiled and said, "Well, here it is: *Cheer up! Roses will bloom again!*" And then the doctor closed his medical bag and left.

A few minutes later, the nurse came into the room. She had been crying because she was so frustrated about having to work with her miserable, bitter, sick patient. She had even asked the doctor to release her from the case, but he had refused. So, she walked back into the room, planning to announce that she was quitting. But then she looked again at the man on the bed.

Suddenly something began to happen in the patient. He began to open his hands. He moved his swollen joints. As the nurse and pastor watched, amazed, the man inched his way over to the side of the bed, put his feet on the floor, and slowly pushed himself up until he was on his feet. As he stood looking around the room, he saw the nurse and smiled at her and said, "Nurse, cheer up! Roses will bloom again!"

Deeply moved by this miraculous change in the man, the pastor slipped out of the room. He drove away, exhilarated and uplifted by the Spirit of God. Later that day, he drove into town to conduct some business. As he parked his car, a friend saw him and approached him.

"Preacher, do you have a moment?" asked the friend.

The pastor replied, "Sure, what can I do for you?"

The man looked downcast. "Well, you know how bad business has been," he said. "I'm in the process of filing for bankruptcy. It hurts. But what hurts me most are the people who have worked for me, some of them for many years. It seems those I have to let go first need the job the most. But what can I do?"

The pastor sympathized, but he wasn't sure at first what to say. Then he remembered what had happened to the arthritic man. He said to his friend, "Listen, I've got good news."

"Well, what is it? Tell me."

"Cheer up! Roses will bloom again!"

Then the pastor walked on down the street and met his congressman. He said, "Hello, Congressman. How are things in Washington?"

"Well, Pastor, I'm sorry to tell you things aren't good," said the congressman. "The deficit is soaring, and nothing seems to work. It looks to me like we're in for some real trouble. This country may fall apart."

The pastor said, "Congressman, haven't you forgotten something?"

"What is that?"

"Roses will bloom again!"

The congressman thought about it. Then he smiled and said,

"You know, I had forgotten the secret of life itself — that roses will bloom again. Thank you, Pastor, you've made my day."

That evening, as the pastor drove home, he decided to visit a young couple whose child had died and been buried a few days before. When he arrived, he found the young father home from work early. His wife sat staring in space. Without lifting her head, she said, "Pastor, do you really believe in life after death?"

The pastor answered, "Yes, I believe in the resurrection of the dead through the Lord Jesus Christ. I believe God will raise the dead."

Again, without lifting her head, the grieving mother said, "Will you please explain that a little more?"

"Well," he said, "in terms of the passing of your little child, yes, your little child lives. He is alive forever with Jesus. But more than that, the resurrection means there will be many new beginnings in our lives here on earth. Many resurrections are going to happen to you and your husband from time to time. You're going to feel inspired, uplifted, strengthened in many ways in the days and years ahead."

The woman still had her head down, full of grief. But the pastor felt the joy of what he had just told her about the goodness of God to give us new beginnings even after the darkest of times, and he smiled. He kept smiling until the young woman looked up as if to say, 'Well, what is there to smile about?' And he said to her, "My dear, roses will bloom again!"

A few weeks later, the pastor returned to visit the sick man, and was surprised to see that the man was no longer in bed. Instead, he was out in the yard doing some light work. He was recovering!

The same day, the pastor ran across his business friend. The friend told him, "Pastor, I'm glad to see you. I've had a turnaround. The last two months have been amazing. Orders have come in from everywhere. I've rehired all my people and even hired new people. We're the only business in this town that's booming like this, and I hope we're the forerunner of many more. Roses are blooming again!"

Encouraged, the pastor decided he would stop by the young couple's house and see how they were. When he arrived, they were there to greet him. They said, "Pastor, how do you think the people will feel if we come back to church on Sunday?"

He said, "They'll feel just great! They've been very concerned about you and have been praying for you."

The young mother smiled. "Look for us on Sunday. Roses are blooming again!"

God Is Not Through Blessing You

If you have ever taken a trip across the deserts of the southwestern United States, or deserts anywhere around the world, then you'll know what I'm describing here. These areas are barren, and they often seem lifeless. Sometimes, it feels like all you see is dirt and sand for miles and miles without a sign of life.

But if you stop and look at the desert more closely, you'll see something amazing. There will be life. Small desert animals will crawl in and out of their little dens. Here and there, the sort of grasses and brush that can grow in sandy soil will make an appearance. If you look even more closely, you may even see a desert rose — a type of rose that grows and blooms in dry, rocky places.

Dad often talked about the time he and my mother had stopped while driving through the desert, and they came upon a beautiful, tiny, delicate desert rose. Dad said that as he stood there, looking at it and wondering how it could grow out of that hard-packed, cracked earth, a scripture came to his mind.

Isaiah 35:1

And the desert shall rejoice and blossom as the rose.

I want to encourage you always to see your situation through the eyes of God. Yes, it may seem like you're traveling through a desert. It may seem as if you're surrounded by barrenness and lack. But if you'll just believe, roses will bloom again.

Friend, it takes God to put the bloom on the rose. But He can do if for you, if you will believe Him. Your faith will give life to you in the desert of your circumstances. Roses will bloom again!

What is God trying to say to you in the midst of your circumstances? He's saying that He's not done blessing you. His miracles are not over for you. Your faith can work again… and again… and again… as often as you need it to bring forth miracles to meet your needs and fill your lack.

Psalm 71:14

I will hope continually, and will praise You yet more and more.

Do you know who spoke the words in Psalm 71? It was King David. And David was a man who understood through experience what it was to have lack, to struggle, to grieve. In his lifetime, David lost his best friend, Jonathan. He struggled much of his life to stay alive, threatened by King Saul, who was enraged by jealousy against him. David spent years hiding in caves to escape the king's persecution. He lost an infant son. He lost a beloved son, Absalom, who had rebelled against him. He lost battles. He suffered sickness and injury. He saw his sons feuding.

Yet David wrote, "I will hope continually."

What did David hope in? He hoped in God. He hoped in God's Word (Psalm 119:81). He trusted God to be true to His Word, even when things looked desperate. He trusted God to be his rewarder, every time tragedy struck him and every time he felt lack.

God does not play favorites. He loves you and has answers for you, just as He loved and had answers for King David. That means there is hope for you.

Your circumstances may seem desperate right now. You may have lost a loved one. You may be suffering with sickness or disease that has left you weak in your body. You may be struggling with debt or financial worries. Maybe you've lost a job, or received terrible news, or you're separated from those you love and you wonder how there will ever be a restoration.

You may need an answer desperately.

But I say to you right now, by faith… God is alive, and He is here. He is present with you in the midst of your circumstances. He's at the point of your need right now. He's ready and willing to work with you to overcome your lack and cause you to thrive.

Don't give up. Keep looking to God to open up a way for you in the desert. And remember, no matter how bad your circumstances may appear, there is hope. Roses will bloom again.

Remember These Principles

- Life is full of challenges — but how we come through them has a lot to do with our attitude.

- It is up to us to choose whether we will focus on the problem at hand, or on the hope for our future that our faith in God offers us.

- No matter how lifeless a situation may seem, all things are possible with God.

- It's important to see our circumstances through the eyes of God…the eyes of faith.

- Don't give up! There is always hope with God. And there are blessings for those who continue to place their hope in Him (Psalm 31:24, Jeremiah 17:7).

CHAPTER SIXTEEN

What's Your Decision?

What about you today?

Has this book inspired and strengthened you in your faith concerning God's desire and plan to meet your needs?

Have you decided to believe what God says about His willingness to supply all of your need according to His riches in glory by Christ Jesus?

Have you committed yourself to coming against your needs through faith in God and in His Word?

Have you recognized that faith is your number one tool in attacking your lack... and that you have the faith you need because God has already given to you the measure of faith so that you can thrive in Him?

Have you accepted God's promise that you can overcome your needs and problems... that you can thrive and live a life that is full and rich and fulfilling?

Have you committed to both give and receive from God, by faith?

Have you started seeing your giving as a seed you sow, expecting back a miraculous harvest from God, who has more than enough to meet your needs?

Have you made God your source? Do you look to Him as the One who will supply all your needs according to His riches in glory?

Have you determined to keep on moving forward in faith, believing that your circumstances will turn around, that roses will bloom again in your life?

Have you determined to give your best seed, and then expect God's best in return?

Have you decided that with God as your source, you are never out of options?

Are you confessing what God says about your situation, rather than what the devil, the world, or others say about it?

If you are answering "no" to any of these questions, go back and reread the chapter that deals with that issue in your life. Read it and reread it until the truth of God's Word gets down deep into your spirit. Continue to speak His Word over your life, expecting miracles.

And never forget…

God wants you to attack your lack and see your needs met. He wants you to thrive in Him. He wants you to have life — a life that is abundant to overflowing with His presence and His goodness.

And so do I.

CHAPTER SEVENTEEN

Summing It All Up

Now that you have read through this entire book, I believe it is time to put what you have learned into practice. There is no better time than right now to start resisting the devil's attacks and coming against any need or lack in your life with your faith in God's Word.

More than anything else, I want to see you prosper in your life! I want you to prosper in your spirit, in your mind, in your body, in your family — in every area of your life, from the crown of your head to the soles of your feet. So, I encourage you to take the following steps to help yourself be strong in the Lord and in the power of His might as you take your faith stand and declare "No more lack!" to your circumstances:

1. Reread this book. Reread it as often as you need to do to get these biblical principles down into your heart where they can build your faith for miracles.

2. If you have been focusing too much on your problems instead of on God, who brings solutions, then repent and ask the Lord to forgive you. According to 1 John 1:9, *If we confess our sins, He is faithful and just to forgive us our sins and to cleanse us from all unrighteousness.*

We all make mistakes. The best way to turn around and start going in the right direction is to ask God to forgive the mistake and ask Him to help you move forward in the right direction from this moment on.

3. Know that it is time to plant seeds of your faith toward filling your life and defeating any lack in it. Whether you're facing needs that are financial, physical, emotional, spiritual, or in your relationships, ask the Lord what seeds you can sow against those needs and do it. Then expect and keep expecting a harvest from the seed you sow.

4. Use the Confessions on the next page to help you build your faith in God concerning your life. Remember, God doesn't want you to experience lack. He wants you to thrive and to walk in His blessings and enjoy an abundant life. Make these confessions daily and watch as your circumstances begin to turn around for your good.

MY PERSONAL "THRIVING" CONFESSIONS

Instructions: Use the following prayers and confessions daily as you take a stand in faith against any needs or lack in your life. Speaking them out loud will help you to hear God's Word, which is where faith comes from. Ask God to show you the areas in your thinking that need to change so that you can get rid of doubt and worry concerning your needs, and expect His abundant provision with faith.

I'm praying for you to thrive and experience God's best in your life... with full provision from His abundant supply... and no lack, in Jesus' Name! —Richard

God's will for my life is that I prosper and am healthy in every area. As I serve Him, my soul prospers, and the lack in my life is filled. *Beloved, I pray that you may prosper in all things and be in health, just as your soul prospers* (3 John 2).

∎ ∎ ∎ ∎ ∎

I am a child of God. God loves me. And He gives me strength to overcome anything. *I can do all things through Christ who strengthens me* (Philippians 4:13).

∎ ∎ ∎ ∎ ∎

The source of lack is the devil. But Jesus came to give me abundant life. As a blood-bought child of God, by faith, I will thrive as I walk in the abundance He has for me. *The thief does not come except to steal, and to kill, and to destroy. I have come that they may have life, and that they may have it more abundantly* (John 10:10).

■ ■ ■ ■ ■

No matter what my circumstances may look like, God's best plan for my life is that I will have a great future filled with hope. *For I know the thoughts that I think toward you, says the Lord, thoughts of peace and not of evil, to give you a future and a hope* (Jeremiah 29:11).

■ ■ ■ ■ ■

I am not a sitting duck, waiting for the enemy to destroy me. Nothing is too difficult for me to overcome when I involve God in my life. *Jesus looked at them and said, "With men it is impossible, but not with God; for with God all things are possible"* (Mark 10:27).

■ ■ ■ ■ ■

When I come to God in faith, seeking His supply for my needs, I expect Him to answer because He rewards those who seek Him in faith. *He who comes to God must believe that He is, and that He is a rewarder of those who diligently seek Him* (Hebrews 11:6).

■ ■ ■ ■ ■

My giving is like a seed I sow. It has a harvest attached to it. The more I give to God, the greater the harvests I expect. *Give, and it will be given to you: good measure, pressed down, shaken together, and running over will be put into your bosom. For with the same measure that you use, it will be measured back to you* (Luke 6:38).

■ ■ ■ ■ ■

No matter what I need — whether it is spiritual, physical, emotional, financial, or in relationships — God can meet my need. He desires to care for all areas of my life. *My God shall supply all your need according to His riches in glory by Christ Jesus* (Philippians 4:19).

As I trust God to meet my needs, I speak His Word in faith over my situation, knowing that His Word produces results. *So shall My word be that goes forth from My mouth; it shall not return to Me void, but it shall accomplish what I please, and it shall prosper in the thing for which I sent it* (Isaiah 55:10–11).

■ ■ ■ ■ ■

My faith is in God, not in material things. I know that as I seek God and put Him first in my life, my needs in every area of life will be met. *Seek first the kingdom of God and His righteousness, and all these things shall be added to you* (Matthew 6:33).

■ ■ ■ ■ ■

Even when my mountain of need looks enormous, I have more than enough faith to attack the need and see it supplied by God. *If you have faith as a mustard seed, you will say to this mountain, 'Move from here to there,' and it will move; and nothing will be impossible for you* (Matthew 17:20).

RICHARD ROBERTS

Richard Roberts, B.A., M.A., D.Min., has dedicated his life to ministering the saving, healing, delivering power of Jesus Christ around the world. God has put a dream in Richard's heart of reaching the nations of the earth for Jesus. Since 1980, he has ministered God's healing power in 39 nations spanning six continents.

In his miracle healing outreaches, Richard has ministered to crowds of over 200,000 people in a single service. Often as much as half the audience responds for prayer to receive Jesus Christ as their personal Lord and Savior. Hundreds and thousands more receive healings and miracles as Richard ministers God's Word and operates in the gifts of the Holy Spirit, especially the word of knowledge.

Richard is the Chairman and CEO of Oral Roberts Evangelistic Association. He and his wife, Lindsay, host *The Place for Miracles* — a half-hour interactive broadcast that reaches out to millions worldwide. On this unique healing program, Richard ministers in the power of the Holy Spirit, praying for those who are sick or hurting in some area of their lives, and often giving specific words of knowledge about how God is touching people with His healing power.

The Place for Miracles has received more than 150,000 phone calls to date from viewers who have reported miracles and answers to prayer.

Richard is a man on fire for God and consumed by the compassion of Jesus for sick and hurting people. His meetings across the United States and around the world are marked by a tremendous move of the Spirit, resulting in all types of physical, mental, emotional, financial, and spiritual healings. Richard says, "Jesus was born to step into a world of trouble and bring healing and deliverance, and that's the call of God upon my own life — to reach out to people in their troubles and heartaches, to pray and believe God, and to bring them His Word of hope and healing."

In addition to his responsibilities at the Oral Roberts Evangelistic Association, Richard also served as President of Oral Roberts University for 15 years. In 2010, he founded the Richard Roberts School of Miracles to help equip Christians with practical, hands-on experience in applying God's Word and His healing power in their own lives and in the lives of others, especially emphasizing how Christians can enjoy a life empowered by the Holy Spirit.

Richard has also authored a number of books, booklets, and other inspirational material, including *Unstoppable Increase, He's a Healing Jesus, When All Hell Breaks Loose,* and *Your Road to a Better Life.*

Richard and his wife, Lindsay, have three daughters: Jordan, Olivia, and Chloe.

Richard Roberts
P.O. Box 2187
Tulsa, OK 74102-2187

www.oralroberts.com

FACEBOOK
@theplaceformiracles

TWITTER
@ORMrichard

INSTAGRAM
RichardRobertsORM

Other books by Richard Roberts:

Your Road to a Better Life

The Return

He's A Healing Jesus

Unstoppable Increase

www.oralroberts.com

For prayer,

call ***The Abundant Life Prayer Group***
at 918-495-7777, or contact us online at
www.oralroberts.com/prayer.

RICHARD
ROBERTS
ORAL ROBERTS MINISTRIES